LAURENCE OLIVIER
A Critical Study

Felix Barker

Spellmount
TUNBRIDGE WELLS

Hippocrene Books
NEW YORK

First published in the UK in 1984 by
SPELLMOUNT LTD
12 Dene Way, Speldhurst
Tunbridge Wells, Kent TN3 ONX

ISBN 0-946771-20-0 (UK)

First published in the USA in 1984 by
HIPPOCRENE BOOKS INC
171 Madison Avenue
New York, NY 10016

ISBN 0-88254-926-X (USA)

British Library Cataloguing in Publication Data
Barker, Felix
  Laurence Olivier. — (Film & theatre stars)
  1. Olivier, Laurence, *Baron* 2. Actors —
  Great Britain — Biography
  I. Title.   II. Series
  792'.028'0924   PN2598.055

  ISBN 0-946771-20-0

Commissioning editor: Sue Rolfe
Series editor: John Latimer Smith
Cover design: Peter Theodosiou/Tina Rowe

Printed & bound in Great Britain
by Anchor Brendon Ltd, Tiptree, Essex

Contents

Photograph Acknowledgements

5, Sasha. 9, 10, 14, Angus McBean. 16, 17, 18, 20, John
Vickers. 12, Coburn. 15, Two Cities Films. 22, British Lion
Films. 23, Norman Gryspeerdt. 24, Eagle Films. 25, 26,
Anthony Crickmay. All are from the author's own collection.
He regrets that the photographers and sources of some cannot
be identified.

One

First Player Of Our Time

The epithet 'great' is a weighty burden for an actor to carry; 'greatest' almost unsupportable. But for many years now Laurence Olivier has been regarded as our greatest living actor and has not had to battle unduly hard to retain the title. He has held it firmly and with becoming modesty on both sides of the Atlantic, and it would be surprising to hear it challenged anywhere in the world.

As long ago as 1946 a Broadway reviewer was referring to Olivier - almost as a matter of course - as the leading English-speaking actor. This was after his phenomenal success with the Old Vic in New York. Not long afterwards a leading British critic asserted emphatically that he was 'pound for pound the greatest actor alive'. In 1977 came a generous tribute from someone who was a close rival. 'The greatest living actor' was Ralph Richardson's description, an accolade he bestowed when talking to Peter Hall, director of the National Theatre.

Richardson had just come back from Brighton where he had been visiting Olivier at his home. His old friend had been ill and had said he would never go on the stage again. Richardson swept this aside, saying to Hall that within a couple of years Olivier would be back to 'knock them all flying'. The prediction of a return to the theatre has proved wrong but, even if it is ten years since he was on the stage, Olivier's position remains secure. He is still the First Player of our time.

There are other contenders, of course. Not now - sadly - Richardson who died last year; but some people might name Scofield, Redgrave or Guinness, and certainly many would vote John Gielgud the highest honours. For years they vied with each other, running neck to neck. As far as I know, Gielgud has never gone quite so far as Richardson in his praise of Olivier though he is on record as saying he considers his Macbeth to be 'definitive' and many years ago he honoured Olivier's Richard III with a symbolic gesture of admiration.

Does the question of supremacy matter very much, and isn't there a kind of vulgarity about a list of precedence? If I throw down this gauntlet on Olivier's behalf (and probably much to his distaste) it is because this little volume cannot avoid being something of a summing-up. On May 22 this year - 1984 - Olivier was 77. Even before his kidney operation last winter he was saying that he no longer had the physical resources or memory for further major roles in the theatre. Othello's occupation's gone - or nearly. Now, you might expect, would be a time for tranquility and the Sussex garden . . . for short visits to London to pay tribute at an old friend's memorial service . . . to write a reflective book on the art of acting . . . and forays into films and television only when a particularly worthwhile part like Lord Marchmain in *Brideshead Revisited* comes along. But Olivier stubbornly refuses to retire completely. 'He will go on!' says his wife Joan Plowright wearily. 'I have to act to breathe', he explains. 'I can only stop if He up there smites me.'

Not a year has passed since he was forced to give up the theatre when he has not appeared in one film for the cinema or television, and the less exhausting demands of studios made a television King Lear possible two years ago. These are welcome returns to brief glory to demonstrate to himself and the world that, though not quite so steady now, his light still shines.

In these circumstances, let us take the plunge and risk comparisons. Sooner or later someone must try to assess Laurence Olivier's place in theatrical history, and perhaps there is already sufficient perspective for us to see if the claim of pre-eminence holds water.

Every age has its First Player. Richard Burbage, Garrick, Kean, Macready and Irving all reigned and then handed on the crown. Early in this century the number of important actors so thickened on the ground that it is not easy to say who - Tree, Forbes-Robertson, Benson? - has the claim to supremacy and in what order. In the United States Edwin Booth gave way to Richard Mansfield, Mansfield to John Barrymore, Barrymore to Alfred Lunt, and for a while there was Orson Welles rumbling threateningly in the wings. But in Britain during the early 1930s a new and undisputed First Player emerged. John

Gielgud took the throne and held it for at least fifteen years. He has never been formally deposed. Olivier has never matched the music and rich beauty of Gielgud's speaking of poetry. But there came a moment when Gielgud's fragile sensitivity melted before the blowtorch heat of Olivier's dynamic personality. That moment arrived in 1944.

In September *Richard III* opened like a clap of thunder and Olivier struck like lightning at the New Theatre in London; the question of precedence came up; and people began to ask if Olivier should be accepted as the greatest living actor. Catching the mood of the public, the papers invited readers' opinions. Critics were canvassed. James Agate sidestepped the question by quoting a Scottish caddie who when asked if Tom Morris or Bobbie Jones was the better golfer replied: 'Baith o' them played pairfect gowf!' Donald Wolfit, who was then performing seven Shakespeare plays and one by Ben Jonson in repertory, and was not noted for humility is said to have conceded that this performance put Olivier at the head of the profession.

Though he probably did not see it as such, Gielgud made a gesture which many people interpreted as settling the matter. He possessed the sword which Irving had worn as Richard III (and before him Edmund Kean). When Olivier opened to huge acclaim, Gielgud was playing at the Haymarket and one evening he sent the sword round to the New. The inscription on the blade said the gift to Olivier came from 'his friend John Gielgud in appreciation of his performance as Richard III'. Perhaps it is a little far-fetched to see this as the symbolic gesture of an abdicating king handing over his sword of state. But from then on it appeared that the British stage had a new First Player.

It is with Olivier the actor that this book is chiefly concerned, but his other achievements cannot be ignored. As one reads down the four closely packed columns of his entry in *Who's Who in the Theatre* there is the bewildered reflection that perhaps he has done almost too much. As a stage director of the first rank, his major productions span forty years from his New York *Romeo and Juliet* in 1940 to *Filumena*, also in New York, in 1980. He first became a manager in 1935 when he was only 28, and fourteen years later leased the now-demolished St James's Theatre determined to bring back the lustre and traditions it

11

had possessed under actor-managers. Though now half-forgotten, and seemingly incidental to his main work, his company, Laurence Olivier Productions, staged plays as varied as the American comedy *Born Yesterday* and Menotti's modern opera *The Consul*. He admits to many financial failures with this company, but amiably explains them away by saying that in a theatrical manager's life 'hope is constantly at odds with his better judgment'. 'Innumerable' is his own description of his film roles. Even he has lost count. His achievements in the cinema with Shakespeare would for any other man be a career in itself. And to all this has to be added the climactic undertaking of his life: Directorship of the National Theatre.

With the advance of the years his hair has thinned and bifocals have bcome a constant necessity. Offstage, Olivier seems to have shrunk. You still half expect to be confronted with the towering resounding hero of Agincourt; instead, rather frail in a neat grey suit, he is now as inconspicuous as a retired bank manager. But when he talks the twinkle comes back into his eye. There is the old trick of dropping his jaw in irony. The penthouse lids still come down over the eyes, now as always, a warning of boredom or suppressed anger. The old charm is still there just below the surface.

If Olivier's height appears to have diminished, his stature has increased thanks to honours heaped upon him. It could be that he is stooping under their weight: knighthood (the youngest actor ever); peerage (the first actor Baron); Legion d'Honneur; honorary doctorates from Oxford and three other universities; to say nothing of such strange-sounding awards as the Yugoslav Flag with Golden Wreath. Hollywood Oscars are numerous enough to serve in the Olivier household as doorstops with Emmys and multitudinous other statuettes as understudies.

Is it possible to condense the achievements and assess the gifts of so diverse a man into 96 pages? We must see.

Two

First Entrances

The association, simmering into rivalry, between Olivier and Gielgud began with the announcement in 1935 that Gielgud was proposing to stage *Romeo and Juliet* at the New Theatre in London (now the Albery) and that as an experiment he would alternate the parts of Romeo and Mercutio with Olivier. The public were not to be persuaded that this was simply a fortuitous idea; they saw it as a challenge by the ambitious rising star. In fact, since he was invited by Gielgud, Olivier could hardly be accused of prompting the confrontation.

As it turned out, honours were just about even. Gielgud, an actor brought up in the romantic tradition, was a lyrical Romeo; Olivier was the ideal Mercutio full of dash and swagger, a young blood who had walked too much in the heat o' the sun and was a little mad. The great question mark hung over Olivier's playing of Romeo, an interpretation about which there are still divided opinions nearly fifty years later. This performance is particularly important in a long-range view of his career because, at the age of 28, and for the first time in his life, Olivier made a complete break with the accepted style for Romeo. In his research for originality, he showed the kind of daring that was to make him so interesting in the future.

Most young actors see Romeo as a lovesick youth pouring out exquisite verse and playing the balcony scene almost as an operatic duet. Not Olivier. To him Romeo was an adolescent Italian of sixteen, dashing and darkly good looking, not a pale and pining lover out of a book of medieval chivalry. He was determined to make Romeo *real* ('a boy practically with conkers in his pocket', he explained to Gielgud). In tousled wig and olive-skinned make-up, he splintered the poetry into fragments to create the impression of a tongue-tied boy. Sometimes he fumbled for words, substituted clumsy impetuosity for grace and brought a torrent of impassioned ardour to the love scene.

As director, Gielgud was worried, but gave him his head. The reception was very much as he feared. Audiences were bewildered by so unconventional a Romeo; most of the critics damning. Reviews scolded him as a ranting roaring Romeo, temperamentally ill at ease, lacking in poetry and authority, prosaic rather than romantic. 'His blank verse is the blankest I have ever heard,' was one verdict. 'He plays Romeo as if he were riding a motor bike', was another.

For an actor in his first major Shakespearean role in the West End of London such adverse criticism was shattering, and Olivier immediately offered to give up the part. His only comfort came from the opinions of fellow-professionals. They were interested to see an actor trying to break the mould. His great friend in the cast, Glen Byam Shaw, was deeply sympathetic. Tyrone Guthrie (though admitting that he did not get full value from the verse) wrote to say that he was 'thrilled and moved' by his speed, intelligence and 'muscularity'. Margaret Webster, an experienced Shakespearean director, advised him to ignore the critics: 'I found your Romeo full of passion, sincerity and beauty'. In one of the few good reviews, the critic and playwright St John Irvine wrote: 'I do not think I wish to see this play again lest my memory of Olivier be dimmed'.

Looking back on this Romeo, people still recall its gusto and impact. Time has probably played its old trick of erasing memories of detailed imperfections to leave behind a general aura of magic. That this performance didn't really come off in no way appears to have inhibited Olivier's progress. Instead of being crushed by a critical failure at a vital point in his career, he probably saw the immense value of being controversial. Unconsciously or deliberately, this shaped his future acting. In his 1935 *Romeo* we can see the genesis of the versatility, showmanship and surprise with which he has jolted audiences ever since. This was the start of a long line of performances in which he put a new edge on old parts or sought out something quirky and unexpected in a new one.

There was little in the upbringing of Laurence Kerr Olivier, born May 22, 1907, in a semi-detached Victorian villa in Dorking, Surrey to make him particularly unconventional or prepare him for greatness. The son of a Church of England clergyman with High Anglican leanings, he did not seem in any way predestined to be an actor. He had no theatrical forebears. There was, however, just a hint of the histrionic in his father's dramatic preaching and in the colourful ritual of his services. Further back, there was talk of undergraduate rebellion. At Oxford, Olivier's father had joined the Oxford University Dramatic Society, became a sceptical Platonist, and appears to have been sent down. There are vestiges here of an individualism he may have passed on to his son.

A move to London came at the age of five. There was a nursery theatre at seven. Parents attended charades played out by Laurence with an older sister and brother as fellow actors. The first definite theatrical influence came in 1916 when he went to a London church school with a strong choral tradition. The headmaster staged end-of-term Shakespeare of high enough order for actresses like Ellen Terry and Sybil Thorndike to attend with apparent enthusiasm. At Christmas 1917, Laurence was in *Julius Caesar* and Ellen Terry's prophetic diary entry was: 'The small boy who played Brutus is already a great actor'.

Laurence enjoyed acting as a schoolboy, made a hit as Kate in *The Taming of the Shrew*, and while at his public school noted in his own diary: 'Played Puck very well - much to everybody's disgust'. For all this, the first intimation of his future only came when his brother went to India and Laurence asked his father if he could follow him as a tea planter. Out of the blue came the reply: 'You are going on the stage'.

This remark has always seemed to Laurence Olivier to have the neat almost false ring of a theatrical curtain line, but it led to his enrolment in a London drama school, the Central School of Speech Training and Dramatic Art. Here he came under the caustic but exhilarating tuition of the principal, Elsie Fogerty. It was Miss Fogerty who, placing a claw-like forefinger in the middle of his forehead, pronounced that there he had a weakness. Olivier believes that his addiction to false noses could well be based on a subconscious attempt to hide this short-coming.

While still a student there were odd performances in seaside repertory, dismissal from the Lena Ashwell Players for giggling (a tendency which plagued him for years) and a £3 a week walk-on in the last straight play at the Old Empire Theatre, Leicester Square where, in his alternative job as Assistant Stage Manager, he succeeded in ringing down the curtain prematurely. These juvenile follies were almost text-book preludes to joining the famous Birmingham Rep.

In the middle of the 1920s the small Birmingham theatre acquired a great reputation under Barry Jackson who had enough taste and private money to risk Chekhov, Ibsen and Pirandello. Here in the nursery of Cedric Hardwicke, Gwen Ffrangcon-Davies and Felix Aylmer, Olivier's career took shape. A grey-flannelled Malcolm in a modern dress *Macbeth*, a hooded Harold in the verse play of the same name by Tennyson, Chekhov's Uncle Vanya, and ruddy-cheeked Tony Lumpkin: these parts were achieved with precocious assurance aged nineteen.

For a young leading man at this time it was almost statutory to have carefully parted Brylcreemed hair and a Ronald Colman moustache. This gave Olivier an appearance unkindly compared to that of a grocer's assistant, but helped him get the lead in a spectacular production of *Beau Geste* at His Majesty's. He was paid £30 a week and, to play the part, sacrificed the role of Stanhope in *Journey's End*. In deep tan make-up and with a matinée idol's profile as the hero of P.C. Wren's Foreign Legion epic, he was almost asphyxiated by stage smoke on the first night. *Beau Geste* closed in a month; *Journey's End* ran for ever. This salutary lesson taught him never to give up the worthwhile for the specious.

There was a short period of struggle with three London flops in a row and eight months of depressingly little work in 1930. During this time he married Jill Esmond who came from a theatrical family and at the time had far more stage experience than he had. He had proposed within three weeks of their meeting but when, after two years, they married, they found they were not well matched. There was to be a son, but the marriage broke up after a few years. Money pressures when he was setting up home were relieved when Noël Coward offered him the part of Victor in *Private Lives*. The deserted prig of a husband was a thin, unrewarding role, but Olivier heeded

16

Coward's advice: 'Look, young man, you had better be in a success for a change'.

After the London run, *Private Lives* crossed the Atlantic and took Olivier to America for the second time (his first had been a brief visit two years earlier when Broadway had given a poor reception to *Murder on the Second Floor*). Coward's play had an even more overwhelming reception at the Times Square Theatre than in London, but the author declined to let it run longer than three months. This was welcome to Olivier because, in the early boom of the talkies, Hollywood was scouting for British accents and, with his good looks, he was exactly the kind of young leading man for which the studios were searching. RKO made the then dazzling offer of £150 a week and he left for the West Coast.

His experiences with such leading ladies as Elissa Landi, Lili Damita, and Ann Harding and his later traumatic encounter with Greta Garbo, we will come to in due course. Of far greater importance in tracing Olivier's rise as an actor is what happened following *Romeo and Juliet* in 1935 and a discussion which took place on the lawn of a house at Hurley in Berkshire.

Three

Noses and Acrobatics

Hurley was the home of Olivier's mother-in-law, the actress Eva Moore, and there one August weekend in 1936 discussion centred round the season Tyrone Guthrie was to direct at the Old Vic in the coming autumn. Guthrie, then in his mid-thirties, already had a reputation as one of the most exciting directors in the English theatre. He had previously had a great success with Charles Laughton at the Vic and for his return he wanted a big central personality. The actor whose Romeo he had admired was the person he hoped to attract, and the bait he offered was a full-length *Hamlet* to be played on unconventional lines.

Olivier had a few qualms. He was twenty nine and the challenge immense. He was at a critical stage in his career, the painful memory of his Romeo reception still fresh. But he was swept along by Guthrie's enthusiasm and his own ambition. He took advice from Harcourt Williams, an Old Vic veteran, and a telephone call across the Atlantic to his friend Ralph Richardson ('I think it's a very good idea, dear boy') decided him. The salary was £20 a week.

A three-week Italian holiday was devoted to mulling over texts, criticism and commentaries, while an added dimension was given to his concept of the part by Dr Ernest Jones, the Freudian psychoanalyst. Jones's theory was that Hamlet delays his killing of Claudius because he feels subconscious guilt that he is 'in love' with his mother. He is worried that his motive for killing his uncle is not the honest determination to avenge his father's murder; it is really the result of thwarted jealousy. In his performance Olivier gave many hints of his guilt complex and that these subtleties probably passed unnoticed by the majority of the audience was not important; what mattered to Olivier was that they provided the chance of a new interpretation, exactly the impetus an intelligent actor needs.

What the audience did perceive, and greatly liked, was a

Hamlet who possessed in full 'the flash and outbreak of a fiery mind'. He was a steely not a willowy prince. There were glimpses of tender spirit, but in the place of pathos and quivering sensitivity (the Gielgud hallmark) Olivier radiated magnetism and physical excitement. As Hamlet, and later as Coriolanus, he brought back to Shakespeare a virility that had been out of fashion for a generation.

Another original approach to Shakespeare - again it had Freudian overtones - was seen in the following season when he came to play Iago to Ralph Richardson's Othello. The resourceful Dr Jones was once more consulted and he came up with the theory that Iago's jealousy was not prompted by thwarted ambition or out of love for Desdemona, but because he had a subconscious affection for the Moor, the homosexual reasons for which he did not understand. Here again was a subtle and unusual idea that an actor found useful, but not a basic motivation to be underlined so that the audience couldn't miss it. There was, anyway, a conspiracy to keep the idea a secret from Richardson whom Guthrie and Olivier feared would disapprove of any hint of perversion.

These early attempts by Olivier to break free from conventional interpretations of Shakespeare continued throughout his career. He was always searching for a new facet in every role, and this carried on right up to one of the last he played: Shylock in his 1970 *Merchant of Venice*. Setting the play in Victorian style and dress enabled Olivier to see the part afresh and transform the Jew into a top-hatted dandy — a Rothschild or a Disraeli.

The danger to be guarded against was, of course, being too clever, to lose the character in the embroidery. In the three important pre-war years when he was establishing his reputation Olivier took care to prevent this. When he came to *Henry V* he and Guthrie would dearly have liked to debunk what they regarded as a glorification of heroic warfare. 'Warlike Harry' was a character whom Olivier disliked and whose 'scoutmaster humour' as he called it, he found repugnant. But in the 1930s it was not as easy as it is now to fly in the face of the Establishment. In the year of George VI's Coronation irony at the expense of royalty was unthinkable at a theatre with the

19

national position of the Old Vic. So he had to drown his prejudices and make what he could of a character of whom he disapproved.

Olivier enjoyed the bilingual love scene with Queen Katharine. The St Crispin speech, however, stuck in his throat. 'But after a while,' he recalls, 'the words worked their own medicine'. Provided he could make the poetry shine and somehow feel the character, his worries disappeared. He came to appreciate that Shakespeare had invested Henry with superhuman splendour by conferring on him the voice of a poet and it was up to an actor to give full rein to the glory of the words.

After one performance Charles Laughton came round to Olivier's dressing room and exclaimed: 'You're *England*!' This flamboyant compliment fired his imagination and we can see how it became transmuted into something very near reality. When he came to make the film in 1943 he seemed so exactly right for the part that to many people he became completely identified with Henry V and the personification of English patriotism.

With *Coriolanus* in the following year, 1938, he again modified ideas he had at the outset. In rehearsal he tried to invest the part with little informal tricks, throwing away lines in the modern realistic style for fear of seeming pompous and insincere. He wanted to make the contemptuous arrogance of the Roman general believable. But the director, Lewis Casson, kept warning him that he would take away from the overall magnificence of Shakespeare if he went for too much low-keyed realism. So he allowed himself slightly more of the traditional Shakespearian manner than he approved. His reward was to have a performance hailed as great for the first time. Cynically he regarded it as a show-off interpretation lacking variety. But one critic's pronouncement: 'There is now no doubt in my mind that the only sign of a great actor in the making in England today is Mr Olivier' can only be good news when you are just thirty one.

His Coriolanus, like his Romeo, Hamlet and Henry V, had the quality of virility and athletic daring which was to become the Olivier hallmark. Like Lewis Waller who precipitated himself onto the stage by pushing off with his foot from the wall in the wings, Olivier delighted in strenuous action. Sometimes this came close to perilous acrobatics. In his 1938 *Coriolanus* (and when he returned to the part in 1959) he took daring to extremes. In the climactic scene at the Old Vic he threw himself down a staircase in a complete somersault, rolled over three times on his side and crashed to final death just short of the footlights. Recalling how this brought up the applause, he determined to outdo the effect at Stratford two decades later. With suicidal frenzy Coriolanus leapt up a flight of steep steps, threw away his sword, and was impaled by a dozen spears of the conspirators. He toppled forward and was only saved from a 12ft headlong drop by being caught by the ankles by two soldiers. He dangled head downwards in a scene reminiscent of the end of Mussolini.

Acrobatics were again on show in *The Critic* at the New Theatre in 1941 when, as the gesticulating Mr Puff, Olivier was hauled into the flies on a painted cloud. Moments later at the play's climax he swung down clutching the front curtain as it fell — an elaborate piece of business which on one occasion he rounded off with a double somersault. He often hurt himself with these stunts but found them irresistible. One of the most hazardous was in the film *Hamlet* when he took a swallow dive down from the balcony to kill Claudius with the cry, 'The venom to thy works!' This was so risky that it was postponed to the very end of filming.

Another of Olivier's preoccupations has always been with make-up. A part might not provide anything particularly new in interpretation, but there would be constant experiments to vary his appearance. Immediately after his clean-cut, handsome Hamlet came a Toby Belch which rendered him unrecognisable. There was a wart-like bridge on a prominent putty nose, pouches under the eyes, bits of sponge wedged in the mouth to create bulging cheeks, and the whole bibulous effect topped off with a straggling moustache. Another false nose, false gums and a yellow pallor which suggested a Macbeth from Outer Mongolia gave rise to Vivien Leigh's classic description: 'You hear Macbeth's first line, then Larry's make-up comes on, then Banquo come on, then Larry comes on'. In a way, she may have been to blame for she had made him a present of Macready's make-up box.

False noses became a trademark, subjects for a joke he latterly told against himself. 'This is my Heroic Nose No 137 - and it itches a bit', he said while filming *Spartacus*. 'I arrived at it though a long process of elimination'. He numbered them off — Romeo, Hamlet, Tony Belch, Macbeth, Coriolanus. 'I didn't for Iago but I did straighten the thing out a bit in *Pride and Prejudice* to give me a majestic look. I wore a nose as Nelson and one for Richard III and two when I did *The Critic* and *Oedipus* on the same night'.

He could have added the inquisitive legal nose for Mr Justice Shallow and — to come — Roman noses of different styles for Antony, Caesar and Titus Andronicus as well as the aggressive military nose for Captain Brazen in *The Recruiting Officer*. One with which he experimented was a prominently Jewish nose for his 1970 Shylock but he discarded it in favour of a more subtle make-up.

James Agate once bewailed the fact that Oliver was 'buried in lime and plaster', and the love of dabbling in make-up has never left him. This culminated in his Othello inspired by the 18th century statue of a Moor at the Ca' Rezzonico in Venice. He distended his nostrils and not only blacked up but polished the patina of his skin to bring it to a sheen. He was greatly disappointed when a noted make-up man said he was sorry but he couldn't make him a pair of rubber lips.

In *Too Many Cooks*, his first film, aged 27

In *Private Lives*, 1931, with Adrienne Allen. N

...ward and Gertrude Lawrence are rolling on the floor.

Left: 'First Larry's make-up comes on' . . . As Macbeth in the
1937 Old Vic production

Above: In *Q Planes*, a film thriller with Ralph Richardson, 1938

27

As Hamlet in the Old Vic production 1937. Vivien Leigh appeared as Ophelia when the play was performed at Elsinore, *left*

As Nelson in *Lady Hamilton* with Vivien Lei

ted in Hollywood by Alexander Korda in 1940

The film that changed Olivier's attitude to films – *Wuthering Heights* with Merle Oberon as Cathy

Four

Return To The Old Vic

When the Second World War broke out Olivier was 35 and, as for so many people, this effectively cut his career in half. The curtain came down on his *Coriolanus* in 1938 and rose on his *Richard III* in 1944. In the interval there were other parts to be played such as a somewhat ineffectual officer in the Royal Naval Reserve and making the film of *Henry V*.

In the summer of 1944 the Governors of the Old Vic applied for Olivier's release from the Fleet Air Arm which was granted, he says ruefully, 'with an alacrity on the part of the Lords of the Admiralty which was almost hurtful'. The interrupted run of successes at the Old Vic was resumed with the resuscitation of the company. The theatre in the Waterloo Road was bombed so it was at the New (Albery) Theatre that Olivier, co-director with Ralph Richardson and John Burrell, planned two unforgettable seasons with fine casts which included Sybil Thorndike, Nicholas Hannan, Margaret Leighton and Joyce Redman.

The first three plays were *Peer Gynt*, *Arms and the Man* and *Richard III*. Olivier had hoped to play Ibsen's mystical hero but Richardson had already earmarked this for himself. So, with seeming modesty, he took the small part of the Button Moulder. This symbolic character has only one short but effective scene towards the end of the play, and, rather as Olivier calculated, this was regarded as self-sacrifice in the true repertory spirit. He was biding his time for Richard. His Sergius in *Arms and the Man*, the Shavian romp between the two major plays, happily served to show his versatility. With curled moustachios and wild, flashing eyes, he played all out for laughs.

If there is one part which assures Olivier's immortality it is his Richard III. Satanic appearance. Savage whip of the tongue. Sardonic humour and icy malevolence. Sly cunning in life; frenzied convulsions in death. He brought an astonishing range of evil to the character and fused them into a charismatic whole. Out of forebodings that he was going to fail sprang a performance which was given an overwhelming first night reception.

In the first great soliloquy which starts:

Now is the winter of our discontent
Made glorious summer by this son of York . . .

Olivier emerged from the shadows, his back half turned on the audience. He closed the door behind him with a sharp click of the lych-bar, then slowly turned to face us. When he spoke his words fell like frozen dew drops – or (more prosaically and as Olivier thought of it) he spoke with the kind of voice old actors put on when imitating Irving. The effect was instantaneous. He felt himself held fast to his audience as if by the convulsions of an electric shock. His variety of pace and the cut-and-thrust delivery never permitted the grip to slacken. There was fearful anticipation of what this limping, treacherous creature would do next.

Olivier started by playing down. This was how he had captured his audience as Hamlet in his first performance at the Vic eight years before. He made us come to him. He avoided the pitfall of making Gloucester too hideous and villainous from the start. Deformity was minimised to a limp and slight stoop (no padded shoulder lump), but the face was evil – tapir-thin nose, wart on cheek, hard lined mouth. His lank black hair was streaked with red. Fellow-actors are said to have avoided him in the wings.

At first we were deceived by his seeming amiability, mesmerised by the smile which flashed on and off with a speed to match his viper tongue. Slowly evil began to accumulate and villainy reached its climax with his acceptance of the crown. Then we were swept through oceans of blood to the Battle of Bosworth and a death scene which was given the full Olivier treatment. After a terrific duel with Richardson's Richmond he went down on the ground. But he wasn't finished. His writhing body shook off Richmond's triumphant foot. It seemed that his black soul might never leave his body. Then in his death agony his eye caught sight of the cross-shaped hilt of his sword. That exorcised the last dregs of evil. He finally collapsed.

This 1944 performance (revived 1949, filmed 1953)

combined high art with a certain amount of low theatrical guile. Unquestionably the total effect was a triumph, but subjected to analysis, revealed a number of devices. For a flying start, Olivier expanded the opening soliloquy to twice its normal length by lifting some of Gloucester's speech from Act III Scene 2 of *Henry VI*. He interpolated two extremely effective lines – the exultant 'Richard's himself again!' and 'Off with his head! So much for Buckingham!' – which are not in Shakespeare but are 18th century accretions by Garrick or Cibber. He raised a laugh by a piece of business borrowed from Emlyn Williams's 1937 performance: while assuming great sanctity in view of the London populus by reading a bible, Richard reveals his pretence by turning over several pages at once without reading them. Then came a touch of acrobatics: the triumphant sliding down the bell rope once assured of the people's acclaim. As for the prolonged death agonies, this was in the full-blooded tradition of Surrey-side melodrama. But these tricks hardly count as blemishes, and one thing is certain: Olivier has copyrighted the part of his lifetime. No other Richard III can escape walking in his crooked shadow.

Five

The Green Umbrella

After the cheers for Richard, Olivier enjoyed a charmed life for the next three years. A series of triumphs crowned his middle years. He was at the peak of his abilities, and he ranged from Shakespeare to Chekhov, Sophocles to Sheridan, finding in each part a memorable quality. Making the transition from 'rooting hog' to the gentle Astrov in *Uncle Vanya* (his role immediately after playing Richard) proved difficult and in the 1945 Old Vic season he did not reach the same degree of perfection that he was to achieve at Chichester seventeen years later.

In rehearsal at the New he found it almost impossible to get to the heart of Chekhov's disillusioned rural doctor, but miraculously, as it seemed to him, he found his clue when making up on the first night. The complexities of the character unified when he first put on the beard and, tilting his head slightly backward, he peered short-sightedly through pince-nez. His appearance was astonishingly like Chekhov himself and at once, and with extraordinary clarity, he saw the part of Astrov as a whole and was able to make him live on the stage.

Actors are quite frequently blessed with shafts of insight such as this. They call it a 'green umbrella' – the help they need, however slight and seemingly extraneous, to find a character and a method of approach. The legendary origins of the green umbrella go back to a German production – some say by Max Reinhardt – when an actor groping hopelessly for an interpretation, appeared one day at rehearsal carrying this particular prop. Immediately the part came right.

Olivier needed the umbrella again, years later, when he had to cope with the baroque complexities of Christopher Fry's verse in *Venus Observed*. By restricting all illustrative gestures to one speech he found the discipline and style he needed for the Duke of Altair. He found, I feel sure, another such clue to character in the single red rose which he brought on for his first entrance as

Othello. Olivier carried no such flower until the dress rehearsal but here was the perfect symbol to help him bridge and reconcile the brutal and romantic sides of the Moor's character.

Sometimes it has been a trick of speech that has provided the hidden spring, the touch of variation he is constantly seeking. He adopted a stammer for Hotspur in *Henry IV* taking the idea from Lady Percy's remark that her husband had a way of 'speaking thick which nature made a blemish'. Other actors have done this, but Olivier chose the leatter 'w' as the verbal impediment. This lent special pathos to his dying words: 'No Percy, thou art dust and food for w-w . . .'and then, struggling vainly to get out the last word, he left it to Prince Hal to finish the sentence with '. . . for worms, brave Percy'. (Hotspur also gave the actor yet another chance for a spectacular death. After Hal's mortal sword thrust, he stood for some moments quite upright, blood from a neck wound oozing through his fingers before plunging forward down two stairs onto his face.)

By following Hotspur with the quavering Mr Justice Shallow in the second part of *Henry IV*, both small roles, Olivier was again displaying his gift for showmanship. At the same time he was preparing the way for an even more daring *tour de force* – the squib of Mr Puff in *The Critic* contrasted with the giant rocket of *Oedipus*. It might be thought showing off to play such different roles on a single night ('Would Irving have followed Hamlet with Jingle?' demanded one testy critic) but the public were delighted with his versatility.

The great cry to which Olivier gave vent when the blinded Oedipus hears that he has married his own mother remains an enduring memory for all who heard it; something unique in theatre history. It has been suggested that his awful sound of anguish must still be resounding in the dome of the theatre. Most texts render the sound as 'Oh! Oh!' but Olivier decided that by changing the sound to a longdrawn-out 'Er!' he could convey greater agony. He was to repeat this same expression of woe in a modern domestic setting in *The Entertainer* when Archie Rice hears of his son's death. With his back to the side of the proscenium he slid tragically down as his cry soared up.

After *Oedipus* Olivier felt ready in the following year for the really big challenge of *King Lear*. Ignoring the warning of what happens to tragic heroes who indulge in *hubris*, he decided to direct as well as act. He said he had so many ideas about the tragedy that if they had to be conveyed through the medium of a director he would be involved in awkward discussions every time he wanted to explain a point to the cast. He preferred to take on the whole thing.

There seems logic in this reasoning, but no little daring as well, and, for whatever reason, he failed to give the supreme performance he had hoped. He was much praised and the word 'great' appeared in some reviews. His Lear was described as unfaltering and unflagging. Such was his reputation by now that there was never an empty seat during the run. But praise was nearly always qualified, and there seemed a concensus of opinion that Olivier was a comedian by instinct, a tragedian only by art. Here was a Lear with a sense of humour! He divided his kingdom among his daughters as if fully aware of the absurdity of what he was doing. His later fears of madness revealed a grimly comic edge. It was also suggested that he was too intelligent, that a Lear like Donald Wolfit's in whom there appeared a streak of animal dumbness, came off better. In the later scenes of downfall and madness he somehow just missed the full tragic impact and he failed to be as moving as he should have been.

Would his interpretation have been better for being simpler – a quality which an independent director might have imposed? Without the diverse production worries would he have been able to give his performance the extra concentration it needed? Looking back, Olivier accepts that he could not hope to bring off everything he wanted in a single rendering. Voicing the constant complaint of actors, he said he wished he had not been judged on his first night. It took him four or five performances before he considered he was doing full justice to Lear.

Six

The Road To Hollywood

The story of Laurence Olivier's conversion to films is now almost as familiar as the religious experience of Saul on the road to Damascus. The date was 1938. The place: United Artists Studios, Hollywood, where the notoriously malapropic Sam Goldwyn was putting *Wuthering Heights* on the screen. Goldwyn had assembled a cast of predominantly British actors, among them Merle Oberon as Cathy, David Niven, Flora Robson and Hugh Williams. Fresh from his first triumphant Old Vic season, Olivier had been imported for the part of Heathcliff, the passionate young gypsy of Emily Brontë's novel. It was good casting and, at the age of 31, he was anxious for international screen fame which would make him able to dictate his future.

As he was later to admit, his approach to Hollywood, to Goldwyn, to the role of Heathcliff and, above all, to William Wyler, the director from Alsace, was disastrous. He squabbled with Merle Oberon, argued with Wyler, and shaped his performance in a way which he considered absolutely realistic but went so far that a badly upset Goldwyn exclaimed: 'His face isn't even clean!' and threatened to close down the picture.

Olivier was not used to being treated like a naughty schoolboy, but he knew that for all his talk about realism his interpretation was a bit slap-dash. He hadn't bothered to evolve a technique of acting to suit the screen. 'Your poor anaemic medium can't take a full-scale performance,' he had sneered at Wyler. But his flare-up with Goldwyn on the set made him appreciate that realism (which he had always preferred to exaggeration on the stage) needed to be even more subtle and refined on the screen because any hint of insincerity is shown up by the camera. He began to listen to Wyler instead of scoffing, to learn from his experience and admire his demand for perfection. In place of a theatrical, larger-than-life 'performance' as Heathcliff he substituted a real person in whom the audience could believe.

Resistance to the demands of the cinema was very usual among actors of Olivier's generation. His birth in 1907 coincided almost exactly with the inception of the movies, and he had grown up regarding them as trivial, even undignified, for a stage actor. Not until the arrival of the talkies in 1929 did he, like many stage people, begin to see that a new world might be opening up for him.

Olivier's early studio experiences were not very inspiring. Starting as an amateur cracksman in a 'quickie' called *Too Many Crooks* in 1930, his career had taken him and his valued English accent to Hollywood. This was immediately after *Private Lives* on Broadway. There, for the first few months, life was new, heady and quite enjoyable. While the rest of America staggered under the impact of the Wall Street Crash, Hollywood was a boom town thanks to the new popularity of talkies. Movies offered the cheapest entertainment available.

In these conditions Olivier made his first American film, a steaming tropical affair with Adolphe Menjou, called *Friends and Lovers*. Noting his moustache and good looks, RKO let it be known that they had a new Ronald Colman up their sleeve. But he disappointed the publicity department by declining to be coaxed into white flannels and represented as the typical cricket-playing Englishman. The film itself was a pretty negative undistinguished affair in which Olivier enjoyed a small success as an army officer on the Indian frontier.

His second Hollywood film, *The Yellow Passport* in which he played an heroic British journalist ('the film industry's greatest compliment to Fleet Street') was not much better even though Elissa Landi made an attractive heroine. Ann Harding, his leading lady in *Westward Passage*, proved a generous actress, even allowing him better camera angles than herself. But he was still glad when Gloria Swanson, about to start a film in England, said she wanted him as her leading man and he was able to return home. The resulting comedy, *The Perfect Understanding*, in which he was a drunken socialite, was, he has always contended, the worst film ever made. Nor did his first experience of filmed Shakespeare help matters. The refugee German actress, Elisabeth Bergner, was to make *As You Like It*, directed by her husband, Paul Czinner, and she asked for Olivier as Orlando.

This turned out to be a sometimes outlandish experience when, if his Rosalind was off the set, he found himself called on to register close-up reactions to what she was supposed to be saying.

When he left Hollywood Olivier was full of good intentions never to return, but he was lured back in 1933 when he received a much-publicised summons to be Greta Garbo's leading man. Here was fame. Or rather, that was how it looked until he arrived at MGM studios to find Garbo remote, strangely unresponsive and his promised part in *Queen Christina* far from assured.

Attempts to play love scenes with her were disastrous. Her reply to attempted off-set small talk was 'Life's a pain anyway!' Within a few days he was informed that he was to be replaced. Garbo had decided to give the part to John Gilbert, who had been her leading man in silent films, but now, nearing 40, and with a broad Utah accent, had suffered an eclipse. It was an act of great loyalty on her part, but this did little to reconcile Olivier to the humiliation. Incensed, he left Hollywood after an interview in which he told a reporter that he regarded films as 'about as satisfying as looking at a Michelangelo fresco through a magnifying glass'.

In the light of all this, Wyler's battle for his soul is of considerable importance for, after 1939, film acting began to play an increasing part in his life. Not until *Henry V* did he begin to regard the cinema as anything like as worthwhile as the theatre, but three films which he made in Hollywood immediately before, and just after, the outbreak of war were highly successful.

Rebecca, directed by Alfred Hitchcock from Daphne du Maurier's novel, won an award as the best picture of 1940, and as Max de Winter, moody husband of the timid wife played by Joan Fontaine, Olivier was as plausible as the part permitted. He was better suited to the arrogant Mr Darcy in *Pride and Prejudice* and made a ballroom entrance with a memorable sneer. The third film, shot just before he came back to England to join the Fleet Air Arm, was *Lady Hamilton*, produced by Alexander Korda as pro-British propaganda. As Nelson, Olivier had to deliver such lines as 'You can't make peace with dictators' and somehow survived the melodramatic cry, 'Look out

Bonaparte! By gad we shall lick you now!'

In what Winston Churchill called his favourite film, Emma Hamilton was played by Vivien Leigh and she and Olivier were married just before shooting began. This was the climax to a romance which had begun in 1936 when they were cast opposite each other in *Fire Over England* and had been thrown into daily encounter on and off the set at Denham. She was young, extremely beautiful and married to a pleasant if rather conventional lawyer. Olivier's marriage to Jill Esmond had never been particularly happy, and now, after an affair which they had kept secret from the public for four years, both were divorced and free to marry. It was the beginning of a famous partnership.

Seven

Shakespeare Without Tears

Just before he left Hollywood after the Garbo debacle in 1933, Olivier was asked to call into the MGM office of the producer, Walter Wanger. To soften the blow, or perhaps because he was genuinely interested, Wanger tentatively suggested that he might like to play Romeo opposite Norma Shearer. This was the part ultimately taken by Leslie Howard. Olivier replied coldly that he did not believe in Shakespeare on the screen.

Few pronouncements have been proved greater nonsense by events that followed. The three Shakespeare films which he directed are Olivier's screen monuments.

Henry V was the right film at the right time. Its genesis (a 1938 script, conceived in the early days of television, which went through many permutations) is complicated. That it should have been filmed when it was – or made at all – was the result of happy chances. When it opened in November 1944, five months after the D-Day landings in France, the film about an earlier English invasion across the Channel seemed to have an uncanny topicality. Could anything have a more appropriately heroic ring than: 'Once more into the breach, dear friends . . '?

Released from his duties of training air gunners early in 1943, Olivier embarked on the first film over which he had supreme control. He was producer, director and star. He also had the last word on the script. He chose to film exteriors in Ireland because here, despite the war, he could assemble men and horses in what he considered 'a really poetic countryside'. The stirring result caught the spirit of the times, and three things contributed to a very imaginative piece of film making.

Most remembered is the Battle of Agincourt in which the charge of the French cavalry was filmed by a camera on a straight half mile of railway track. This dramatic and pictorial highlight was inspired, as Olivier acknowledges, by the cavalry charge across the ice in Eisenstein's *Alexander Nevsky*. The second notable feature is technical – reversal of the usual cinema technique of moving in from long-shot to close-up when an actor has a big speech. In Henry's address to the troops before Harfleur the camera starts in close-up as he begins: 'In peace there's nothing so becomes a man / As modest stillness and humility'. Then on the line 'But when the blast of war blows in our eyes . . .' the camera draws slowly back until, on the climactic 'Cry God for Harry, England and St George!' the whole English army is ranged before us.

Controversial – and still a matter of debate – is the mixture of visual styles which were used to blend poetry and realism. The opening (quasi-realistic) employs models to give us an aerial view of Shakespeare's London and zooms in on the Globe Theatre, Bankside. In progress here is a broad Elizabethan-style opening (artificial) to the play *Henry V*. The actors, rouged and bombastic, merge into 'real' people but these historical characters are often seen against formalised two-dimensional backgrounds (unrealistic) purposely designed to suggest medieval paintings. These stylised settings change (to the completely realistic) for the Agincourt battle scenes.

Some people thought this confusing and aesthetically unacceptable. It could also be regarded as a device to save money. Olivier's contention is that the varying styles were essential to make poetry 'acceptable' to the audience. It has to be admitted that the effects do not blend visually, but the tremendous overall impact of this epic film makes the incongruities relatively unimportant.

When he decided to film *Hamlet* five years later, Olivier banished the stylistic confusions of *Henry V* and simplified both his technique and the story of the play. He called it 'An Essay in Hamlet' and by squarely stating in the prologue that this was the story of a man who could not make up his mind, he hoped to overcome objections that he knew purists would raise to the considerable cuts he had made. The simplification indicates that among the lessons he had discovered about film-making one of the most important was that cinema audiences can only take in a limited amount.

The whole presentation was subdued and unified by shooting in black and white. Olivier thought colour was too 'pretty-pretty' for tragedy and he wanted, anyway, to use a small mobile camera (as opposed to a more cumbersome Technicolor one) so that he could keep the action fluid. He planned to dart in and out of scenes and 'track' stealthily from long-shot to close-up which would avoid too much cutting. Black and white also meant he could use deep-focus photography to heighten the film's poetic quality.

At 39, Olivier might have been considered too old for Hamlet (though Irving went on with the part into his sixties) and he himself thought he was just about at the top age. But his name was needed at the box-office and also (as with his stage *King Lear*) he had so many personal theories about the part that he didn't want to have to instil them into another, younger Hamlet.

In a film which displays many original ideas one of the most effective is the way Hamlet's brooding introspection is suggested. To emphasise that it is a thing of the mind, a soliloquy like 'Oh that this too, too solid flesh would melt' is not spoken: it is delivered over Hamlet's pensive profile. The opening lines of the 'To be or not to be' speech are similarily spoken 'over image'. Thus the artificiality of talking aloud at excessive length is avoided.

Naturalism and restraint are the keynotes of the central performance. For the first twenty minutes Olivier holds himself completely in reserve. His face, full and pale and enlarged by the blond cropped hairstyle, registers few variations of expression. Hamlet is often in shadow or with his back turned to the camera. We are being kept at our distance. Fear of theatrical exaggeration – the lesson learned in *Wuthering Heights* – appears to dominate his performance to such an extent that we often feel somewhat denied. The speeches are not as full-blooded as we would like.

This is consistent with the idea of simplifying the complexities of Hamlet's character. Drastic cuts for which Olivier was criticised include 'Oh what a peasant slave am I'. We are left with the impression that this is a Hamlet so numbed by misery that he has lost contact with ordinary human feeling. His voice remains quiet, his emotions suppressed, until the defiant challenge to Horatio – 'I'll rant as well as thou' – at Ophelia's graveside. A criticism one would never have expected to level at Olivier is that he so dampens down outward passion that he is in

Henry V. Above in the 1937 Old Vic stage production and, *right*, in the 1944 film

Astrov in the 1945 production of *Uncle Vanya*. Olivier repeated
the role seventeen years later.

Left, Richard III, Old Vic, 1944

Mr Justice Shallow in *Henry IV* Part II

In the film *Carrie*, 1950

The School for Scandal, in which Olivier played Sir Peter Tea Zealand in 1948 and was se

Vivien Leigh, Lady Teazle, first toured Australia and New
London the following year

danger of disappointing his audience.

The film of *Richard III* needed even more simplification – whole scenes were lifted out bodily – but with a bloody melodrama purists did not voice the same concern about fidelity to text. Olivier appears to have thought that he must make the devil draw in his horns. Again he disciplines the excesses of the theatre to the needs of the cinema. Even his make-up is less extreme than it was on the stage ten years earlier. Fearing that the camera can stand only so much double-dyed villainy, he enlarges the comic dimension of the character. He invites laughter as well as hisses. There is a twinkle in his dark-rimmed eyes as he kills his victims. 'Off with his head!' he orders with a smirk, but suddenly we feel a sickening chill. There is something very frightening about this levity. Mass murder and madness.

Has Olivier succeeded in persuading the public that Shakespeare is proper stuff for the cinema? *Hamlet* won five Oscars. It was voted best film of the year in 1948 by the American Academy of Motion Picture Arts and Sciences and Olivier received the best performance award. Despite Rank's fears, the film made money and has been making it ever since, now largely on the university and art cinema circuits. *Richard III* achieved an unprecedented initial killing. On a single night – March 11, 1956 – the film was shown on television by 146 stations in forty five American states. Viewed by an audience of something like 40 million people, it is calculated that on that one night it had a larger audience than in all the 352 years since its original performance. Olivier was delighted at the initial payment of £250,000 that this brought in, but was not amused at three commercial breaks made by the sponsors, General Motors.

In 1966 Olivier's stage *Othello* became the fourth of his Shakespearean plans to be filmed. This was a straightforward record of the Old Vic production which it is valuable to have even though a few of his more passionate outbursts are so violent and taken at such a pace that the words are lost. Television has captured his *Merchant of Venice* and the recent *King Lear* which, though it falls short of the power that it would have had before his various illnesses, is a most interesting, often moving, record.

One other Shakespeare film remains in the limbo reserved for cinema ghosts. The script he prepared must still be somewhere, but his *Macbeth* was never made. Olivier undertook an expedition to Scotland to choose locations. Conflicting rumours were followed by a formal announcement that the film was to start. On another occasion he grew a beard for the part while wheeling and dealing went on behind the scenes. The hoped-for shooting never began. For years this continued to be a constantly beckoning and receding mirage overtaken by several inadequate versions by other people. Olivier's *Macbeth* is his one great unfulfilled ambition.

Eight

His Own Shop

Playgoing during the years when Olivier was growing up was dominated by the last of the great actor managers. Several were titled, a number had their own theatres. He had always hoped that one day he would follow in the tradition of these childhood gods. It would be very grand if, like Wyndham or Waller, or Tree at His Majesty's, he could 'open his own shop'. His knighthood in 1947 revived the idea, and, while he was looking round for a theatre after the Old Vic tour of Australia, the St James's became available.

A beautiful early Victorian playhouse with an intimate gold-and-red-plush atmosphere, the St James's had been made famous by Sir George Alexander at the turn of the century; here as a nervous boy Olivier had called at the stage door to see Sybil Thorndike; and at 17 had been summoned to the theatre to be interviewed by Sir Gerald du Maurier about a job. Now the cycle of life could be completed. He duly leased the theatre, and in 1950 opened with *Venus Observed*.

Felicitously, this elegant verse play by Christopher Fry provided him with the role of a duke, a man of exquisite taste and sensibility who lives in a house of Georgian splendour: a suitable reflection of his new position. The play was too expensive to stage, and during the next four years the St James's was a luxury on which its loving new manager expended a great deal of money. He insisted on a six-piece orchestra to play in the intervals: canned music would be an abomination. Shoes were hand-made for his actors; hairdressers attended his leading ladies back-stage; nothing but the best would do for Sir Laurence Olivier's regime at the St James's.

The problem, of course, was to find plays to match all this gilded splendour. Just when his business manager was looking particularly grave, Olivier pulled off one of those interesting *coups de théâtre* that have always distinguished his work. He produced Shakespeare's and Shaw's plays about Cleopatra in double harness. Vivien Leigh was the Egyptian queen in both and he alternated Shaw's ageing Caesar with Antony 'the strumpet's fool', whom he did his utmost to invest with the nobility which the Shakespearean scholar, Dr Dover Wilson, wrote to tell him was so essential.

Once he had their measure, he found neither roles particularly rewarding and though the plays were a great success it was impossible to make them pay in a theatre seating only 950. This set a pattern of anxiety for the four years during which Laurence Olivier Productions staged an opera by Menotti and plays by such playwrights as Dennis Cannan and Tyrone Guthrie in a gamble to make both the company and theatre pay. With a visit by the Comedie Française and productions starring Jean-Louis Barrault and Orson Welles, the St James's attained all the prestige for which Olivier had hoped; it remained a bastion of a different age, a nostalgic reminder of the comfortable past. But the pretty little playhouse in King Street was the kind of theatre that was soon to feel the biting wind from Sloane Square and Stratford East, and be looked on with contempt by playwrights and directors with very different social attitudes. Three years after Olivier's lease ended the St James's Theatre was demolished.

The period of being an actor-manager coincided with a lifestyle which not a few people criticised as verging on the regal. The exquisite little Chelsea cottage and Notley, the 13th century Oxfordshire Abbey – his and Vivien Leigh's homes – were a bit grand. This did not worry the public who rather like their gods to be remote beings living on a higher, more luxurious plane. But many people in the profession who were not intimates of the small 'court' in which 'the Oliviers' lived were jealous of their enormous success. They did live well, though not ostentatiously, and never on the scale of great Hollywood stars of the past. There was never any danger that affluence would interfere with hard work. This was important to both of them and necessary if they were to earn enough money to do the plays they thought important.

After taking the Cleopatra plays to New York where they were acclaimed, and staging Terence Rattigan's comedy *The Sleeping Prince* Olivier decided that a return must be made to 'some serious work'. It was about four years since he had embarked on a new Shakespeare role and in 1955 Stratford-on-Avon offered him three plays. One of them, *Macbeth*, directed by Glen Byam Shaw, was his second chance, after a lapse of eighteen years, to have what he called 'a bash at this impossible monster'. At 48 he believed he had the range of vocal effects he needed.

As Macbeth, Olivier showed us once again how effectively he could vary absolute stillness with agility, quietness with sound and fury. He played the opening scenes in a low key as in *Hamlet*, but for a different reason. As Hamlet he had simply been employing the clever actor's trick of slowly drawing the audience to him rather than going out to capture them with big extrovert display. One of the problems of making Macbeth effective as a tragic hero is that he shows his greatest power at the beginning when he is plotting and obsessed with vaunting ambition. After Duncan's death he just goes downhill, drained of strength and purpose. To counterbalance this fault in the play's construction, Olivier started extremely quietly. One of the few flourishes he permitted himself was a grand gesture when in the banqueting scene he confronted Banquo's ghost by leaping onto the table in a billowing scarlet cloak.

From then on he slowly but firmly built up the part bringing all his immense vocal strength to compensate for weakness of character. By the time he came to 'I 'gin to be a-weary of the sun', and was swaying with grief he reached a crescendo of despair. No need this time for the elaborate make-up of former years: he had it all inside him. It was then that he began to plan the film he was never to make.

This Macbeth followed a wickedly funny Malvolio, pasty-faced and with a piss-elegant accent that betrayed him as a preening upstart. Then for the final play of the season, Peter Brook directed him in *Titus Andronicus*. This red, lurid wreckage of a bloodplay had never before been performed at Shakespeare's birthplace. Excluded from the syllabus of polite schools, the melodrama has generally been burlesqued on the rare occasions it has been presented. These were reasons enough to determine actor and director to stage it with complete integrity. The excess of stabbing, killing, strangling, hanging and dismembering must somehow be made believable. Brook supplied barbaric music and a towering sombre setting in which the horrors could be formalised: Olivier made Titus a thick-tongued Roman general so torn with anguish that laughter was impossible. His battle-scarred weariness carried so much conviction that the audience shared his sorrow at the mayhem with which he was confronted.

At Stratford this Titus came within an ace of being a fine performance, but it still needed the refinement that could come only by steering the play through the sea of uncertain reactions provided by various audiences. After a tour in Europe and when the play came briefly to London Olivier was giving a supreme definition of an embattled target of the gods.

Nine

At The Kitchen Sink

While playing Titus, and at the height of his fame as a classical actor, Olivier embraced a new faith: the kitchen sink school of drama. He went to the Royal Court in 1957 to play the broken-down comic, Archie Rice, in John Osborne's *The Entertainer*. This revolutionary decision was to make a considerable change in his career over the next three years.

Various influences were at work, both personal and professional. His marriage to Vivien Leigh was under severe pressure. She had a series of breakdowns, and her increasing instability was making their relationship very difficult. There was an instinct to cut loose from the world and the kind of theatre that their partnership represented. He had a sudden disagreeable vision of himself as pompous, patronising and self-satisfied. But he had not lost all sense of self-criticism. Sensibly he realised that in middle age an artist should stop repeating old tricks. He must come to grips with new ideas.

His wish to break away from the theatrical Establishment in which he had become entrenched made him approach Osborne through George Devine, an old friend and artistic director of the Court. He accepted the play, he recalls, on the strength of the first act. So was born Archie, the red-nosed, blue-jawed variety comic in a grey bowler, tap dancing and telling awful jokes in a twice-nightly nude revue. Olivier went to the Royal Court for £50 a week and created a sensation with his bravura performance. The public knew nothing of his inner motives or his growing attachment to Joan Plowright who played his daughter, an actress of a younger generation with a more socially conscious theatrical background. They simply saw this as one more example of Olivier's astonishing virtuosity, his delight in being capricious. There were rumblings that the dignity of the theatre was betrayed, but also a contrary view that he was wise to make a break with tradition.

The Osborne was followed by another play at the Royal

Court, an even more avant-garde comedy, *Rhinosceros*, by Eugene Ionesco. In this he was a simple soul in a totalitarian world, a tippler who tries to ward off the growth of a horn on the forehead that afflicts all his friends. It was a symbolic view of how the author's native Rumania became tainted under Nazi occupation. Olivier made the struggling little individualist endearingly humble, but this gesture to the Theatre of the Absurd was a further step in the breaking of the old mould rather than a personal success.

The widening of the breach with the past was less successful with *Semi-Detached* which came rather later. The play had been successful in Nottingham and Olivier saw the role of a Midlands insurance agent as another chance to shed his knightly image. He put on a bogus-refined accent and wallowed in the vulgarity of Fred Midway whom he invested with a facial twitch, horn-rimmed spectacles and receding hair. Perhaps he saw in David Turner's comedy a scathing satire on the Welfare State; more likely he thought it a good vehicle in another unaccustomed style. What he failed to perceive was that it would come over as condescending snobbery. He and the play were heavily criticised and he paid the penalty for one of his few errors of judgment. His name kept it going for the eighteen weeks of sheer torture. Every night he felt waves of antagonism from his audience.

The catharsis purged and purified over a period of three years. Part of the process was a complete change in his personal life. Early in 1961 his marriage to Vivien Leigh which had soured so badly during the previous few years ended in divorce, and he married Joan Plowright, who had become a new fount of inspiration. About twenty years younger than Olivier, she was an actress of great quality who not only had an important influence on his career; together they started a new life and a new family in a new home. The kitchen sink seemed of rather less consequence when viewed from the perspective of a Regency house in Brighton, and in 1962 he was ready to return to the kind of theatre in which he was more at ease. He was invited to become director and to open the Festival Theatre at Chichester. This was conveniently near to Brighton and the chance of running a new theatre seemed, as he put it, 'exactly what the dear doctor had ordered'.

In his enthusiasm for the new venture he voluntarily lopped £2000 off the £5000 annual salary he was offered. A company of old friends and bright new players were assembled on the open stage of the circular white building. A policy had to be decided, plays chosen. From the start the project was infused with the excitement and authority that Olivier gives to nearly everything he touches. His involvement at Chichester even extended to his voice, speaking in sepulchral tones over loudspeakers, requiring people to return to their seats at the end of the intervals.

Something unusual, exciting yet traditional, was needed for the opening. A little known play, *The Chances*, by John Fletcher was unearthed in the British Museum. This was followed by John Ford's *The Broken Heart*, another Jacobean play. The third choice was *Uncle Vanya*. Olivier directed all three.

Tyrone Guthrie, Olivier's early mentor, was a powerful advocate of the open stage. It was his ideas that inspired and shaped the new theatre, and he who had suggested to Chichester that they should invite Olivier to be director. Dispensing with the proscenium arch, and having people sitting on three sides of the thrust stage, makes a welcome release from conventional shackles; but Chichester was to have tricky acoustic problems and the width of the stage seemed to demand crowds and pageantry to fill it. The theatre suited a romp like *The Chances* but how would it be for the small-scale subtleties of Chekhov? *Uncle Vanya* was taking a risk, but Olivier wanted to show that the arena stage had the versatility to suit a play conceived for an entirely different sort of theatre and acting style.

At first it seemed a lost battle. Looking down from our seats in the crescent-shaped amphitheatre, we felt like gods observing distant mortals. Chekhov's rural Russians of the last century were so remote that they might have been creatures on a different planet. But Olivier's sensitive direction focused our attention so closely on these civilised tragi-comedy figures of provincial life that they grew in dimension. Soon we were sharing the emotions of Michael Redgrave's nihilistic Vanya, Joan Plowright's love-starved Sonya and Olivier's whimsical, very human Astrov.

In a career which has so often demanded big effects Olivier

had had all too few chances to play quiet naturalistic parts like the country doctor. He made us realise that Astrov was the loneliest man in the world as he travelled aimlessly, endlessly on his rural rounds. There was no direct call for sympathy: on the surface his Astrov was apparently cheerful. Yet we felt an aching sorrow for him in his hopeless passion for Ilyena. There was something immensely touching in the way he positively shed the years as he explained to her the plans he had drawn to illustrate the history of the forests. The doctor was well aware that his hobby was boring to others, but he made us share his enthusiasm as he did his utmost to convey it to the woman he secretly loved.

Astrov was the most subdued performance I can remember from Olivier. He integrated the part with effortless authority into his perfectly orchestrated production. When I reviewed it, I made no bones about admitting that I had been brought to tears by one of the most moving experiences I could recall in a lifetime of playgoing.

It is an extraordinary paradox that, as we learnt long afterwards, the whole cast started that first Chichester performance of *Uncle Vanya* expecting disaster. Olivier even feared they might be booed. They were all amazed by the intensity of concentration and the reception they were given. The play was so successful that it was revived the following season and when Olivier left Chichester to start the National Theatre at the Old Vic in 1963 it automatically became part of the repertory.

Ten

At The National

When he arrived in the Waterloo Road, bringing with him a nucleus of people from Chichester, Olivier began to recruit a company of fifty for the National Theatre. He did so expecting that the new building proposed for the South Bank, would be ready within five years. The Old Vic, where rehearsals started for the opening production of *Hamlet*, was to be just an interim address. It was a wildly optimistic hope for a National Theatre first proposed in 1848 and subject to innumerable subsequent delays. The foundation stone for the South Bank building which had been in position since 1951 was a forlorn joke. Lack of Government funding led to postponement after postponement.

Building did not start until an occasion known as the Ceremonial Cement Pouring in 1969. Olivier couldn't be present: he was getting on with the job of running the still homeless National Theatre Company of which, by then, he had already been the director for seven years. But he sent a telegram. 'How grateful my profession will be for what will ensue from this day's work,' was his message which suggests caution if not actual irony. But as more time passed, he had good reason to feel let down by events. As things were to turn out, the delays spread over fourteen years of his administration were to cheat him of the ultimate achievement of opening the South Bank building. When the theatre which he had planned as the grandest and best ever built was finally opened in 1976 he was no longer the director. Illness and other circumstances had forced him to stand down.

There is a sadness about this, but it must not obscure all that he did achieve during his regime. The plays he put on and the parts he took are a better memorial than any theatre. From the start he surrounded himself with the best people he could find and filled them with enthusiasm and hope for a brilliant future at the National. With a perfect sense of occasion he made the first production a full-length *Hamlet* which he directed as a riot of golden splendour. That night in October 1963, Kettle spoke to Trumpet, Trumpet to Cannon. And Cannon not only to Heaven but to Lambeth and the whole of London. Echoes went round the world.

All was not perfect with the production in which Peter O'Toole decided that Hamlet was some kind of Elizabethan Jimmy Porter, an angry young crank. But there was a glory in the air and from this resounding opening flourish developed years of outstanding productions. In his ten-years regime between 1963 and 1973 Olivier was to launch seventy productions of which he appeared in nine and directed seven. We can concentrate on only a few. Of those in which he acted, *Othello* has a pride of place. He timed it to coincide with the 400th anniversary of Shakespeare's birth.

Because he had always thought that the part called for a deeper voice than he possessed, Olivier had waited a long time before tackling the last challenging peak in his career. Bellowing by himself round the National's rehearsal room in Aquinas Street he forced his voice down to the 'dark black, violet velvet bass' he wanted. His Othello had an arrogantly pursed lower lip and slightly thickened accent. Bare-foot throughout, with an outward splaying of the hands and a Negroid gaucherie in the set of his shoulders, he moulded the outer form of the man. Most white actors are content to black up, often very lightly, and then rely on the poetry and the audience's suspension of disbelief to sustain the illusion. Olivier went for an Othello black in body, heart and soul. Only in the tremendous 'Farewell the tranquil mind' speech did the heroic English actor break through as he sacrificed character to pace and passion. But he quickly reverted to a primitive savage creature with a thin veneer of civilisation.

Less concerned with the 'noble' Moor than a plausible one, Olivier made him suspicious from the start which helped to dispel the usual doubts about how Othello is so easily duped. It was a magnificent performance and when at the end he swayed in terrible anguish with Desdemona's dead body clasped in his arms we, too, were on the rack. It was the quintessence of tragic acting.

Of the several times I saw this great Othello, the most interesting reaction was when the National Theatre took the play to Moscow. The reception at the Kremlin Theatre makes enthusiastic a pale word. At the fall of the curtain the audience swept down the central gangway in a great human tide. They stood three deep along the front of the stage hurling flowers and clapping, many with hands above their heads. A Russian woman in front of me sat with tears running down her cheeks. There were thirteen curtain calls, twelve minutes of standing applause.

It was a reception slightly at odds with Olivier's actual performance. On this occasion he overdid it. The Negroid characterisation (which had come in for some criticism in London) was too extravagantly stressed. His acting, normally perfectly pitched, soared into the realms of the histrionic. Actors, like athletes, probably need a period of acclimatisation after travelling abroad. He was, I think, too keyed up after days of technical problems and carried away by a sense of the occasion. The performance was purposely exaggerated to please an audience most of whom would not be able to follow the English text. An overall impression was more important than subtleties.

Even more incomprehensible must have been Congreve's Restoration dialogue in *Love for Love* which, greatly daring, the National actually opened in Moscow. But the audience responded ecstatically to a piece of inspired business by Olivier's Tattle, the 'half-witted beau, vain of his amours'. When the mincing fornicator makes his escape from an upstairs bedroom window he slides down a roof and, in dishevelled wig and clothes, runs along a narrow wall balancing himself like a tightrope walker. Coming to a wide gap this uncertain tomcat pauses, closed his eyes in silent prayer . . . and jumps. That would be funny in any language. Moscow adored it.

Mr Tattle was a portrait to put alongside another Restoration character, Captain Brazen in Farquhar's *The Recruiting Officer*, one of the National's early successes. This was the actor's Sergius run to seed but sporting the same arrogantly curled moustache. With his lecherous, drink-heavy eyelids, his ravaged jowl and saddle-sore gait, he was immensely funny but kept his portrait this side of caricature. It was another example of restraint (so admirable for Astrov and for Solness in the early scenes of *The Master Builder*) which is an important quality in Olivier's acting but which, unfortunately, has been rationed because so many big parts have demanded big effects.

One such almighty storm lifted the roof in Strindberg's autopsy of love-hatred within marriage, *The Dance of Death*. Olivier was out to wring our withers and he did. His monstrous army captain, Edgar, bullies and blusters as he plots against his wife. Sweating and sardonic, with close-cropped Teutonic head, he went so close to the top that in some scenes he could not fail to topple over into melodrama – a fault which he corrected on the screen. There was one scene in particular when he pursued his wife, whom he suspected of adultery, cleaving the air with his sword and letting out a wild, terrible cry. To me this seemed no turn-of-the-century Swedish military man: it was Othello in white face.

Probably the crescendos varied in intensity on different nights and as Edgar is one of Olivier's favourite parts he must have been pleased by the praise of fellow actors whose judgment he values more than critics'. Gielgud considers it his best non-Shakespearean role, and there can be no disagreement with another verdict that his Edgar 'stays in the mind for ever'. In Olivier's mind the play also holds a permanent and extremely unhappy memory because during the run of *The Dance of Death* he collapsed. People at the theatre had put a look of strain down to the pressure of exhausting parts and disagreement with two colleagues at the National. But the truth was far worse. In June 1967 he was found to have cancer. His treatment at St Thomas's, which he attended as an out-patient so that he could continue acting and directing, was completely successful, but this was the start of a series of other illnesses which have plagued him ever since.

Eleven

Preserved On Celluloid

Olivier let out the news of his first illness only after he had beaten it. This was in 1968 during the filming of *The Shoes of the Fisherman* in Italy. He played a Russian Premier, a beautifully economical portrait in his gallery of screen characters, and one of many parts he has been happy to take without being the star.

Up to this time he had been in more than forty films: since then he has been in almost as many. In a great number he took a small cameo role and polished it fastidiously. He has come to find that a film involving a few days work testing his capacity for creating instant conviction has often been preferable to the more sustained studio commitments.

Among nightmares was the involvement with Marily Monroe. This arose partly from a desire to startle the public and partly because he thought it would be amusing to appear with the world's most vaunted sex symbol. As shooting began just a month before the opening of *Richard III*, he could never again be accused of standing on dignity.

The Prince and the Showgirl proved not at all amusing. He found Marilyn Monroe, temperamental, almost psychopathically unpunctual, and virtually impossible to direct. Somehow he kept his patience and – Svengali to her Trilby – brought out a performance of bubbling freshness. In this screen version of Rattigan's *The Sleeping Prince* she was the Edwardian chorus girl, and he repeated the role he played on the stage of the monocled autocratic Grand Duke. He made the character slightly younger and more romantic as a concession to the cinema, and when he came to film *The Entertainer* he again scaled down his performance. He knocked ten years off the age of Archie Rice and made him less seedy so that his affair with the young girl, Shirley Ann Field, would be more acceptable.

If Archie Rice on the screen never quite touched the heart, another middle-aged failure, the school master in *Term of Trial*, was far more successful. This wife-ridden north country teacher

Hamlet in the 1947 film, which Olivier also directed, with
Felix Aylmer as Polonious

Archie Rice in *The Entertainer*. This is from the film version of the play

Olivier directing Joan Plowright who played Masha in the film
version of the National Theatre production of Chekhov's
Three Sisters

As Othello with Maggie Smith as Desdemona in t‍[

version of the National Theatre production

The Nose that Never Was. Olivier's trial make-up, *above*, with beard, curled forelock and semitic nose which he discarded in favour of the dandified, top-hatted Shylock, *right*, in *The Merchant of Venice*

develops an obsession for a schoolgirl (the young Sarah Miles at her most devastating) and finds himself in court wrongly accused of assaulting her. The impassioned speech he makes in his defence – it was filmed without camera tricks and with the minimum of inter-cutting – was extremely moving and in the actor's most telling manner: deeply felt and understressed.

Again in *Bunny Lake is Missing* there is a demonstration of what can be done with a part, apparently unrewarding, which most actors would regard as a routine exercise. The police inspector investigating a child kidnapping is a mundane figure climbing in and out of police cars and talking over the intercom. But with innumerable little touches Olivier turned him into an interesting character, a policeman with the wisdom of ages under his calm brow. The short haircut, minor public school tie, double-breasted jacket, the walk of someone who probably had once been in the navy: all these contributed to his portrait of a man who was humane under his official coolness. With a fleeting smile for a private joke, he was stolid but never dull. Here is screen acting which is great in its own terms, and it is interesting that Olivier's apparently effortless performance, in fact, is very hard work. To give the impression of free-wheeling on the screen perhaps you need to be beating your brains out – as Olivier was at the time – twice a week on the stage as Othello.

After *Bunny Lake* in 1965 Olivier did not appear in a starring part in a major film for eight years – until *Sleuth* in 1973. In this thriller of international appeal, he had the best comedy role of his screen career as the wealthy, urbane author who is involved in a battle of wits with a hairdresser played by Michael Caine. Hardly off the screen for the whole of the 138 minutes, he is sybaritic and slightly epicene, the master of the sardonic epigram. He varies smooth banter with savage venom when his carefully composed eau-de-cologned face becomes as red as a turkey cock's.

In its way this was as good as anything Olivier has ever done on the screen and led him into a professional duel with Caine, an

Left: The storm scene in the Granada Television *King Lear* with John Hurt as the fool.

actor with a very different background. Caine, the wide boy, with the Cockney accent, is in sharp contrast to Olivier, the polished man of the world: New Cut and Old Vic mesh together perfectly.

The ability to turn in a performance of authority that goes straight to the heart of character is particularly valuable as was seen when in the late 1960s, and ever since when, for health reasons, small parts have been about all he was able to undertake. Many stick in the mind: the silk-tongued, mystical Mahdi in *Khartoum*, the bone-headed, casually adulterous General French in *Oh! What a Lovely War*; Wellington, the stiff jointed old campaigner in *Lady Caroline Lamb*; the desperately tired Air Chief Marshal Dowding in *The Battle of Britain*; the Dutch doctor pleading with the Germans for a truce in *A Bridge Too Far*.

The same incisive quality and uncanny assumption of an alien personality were seen in two larger roles in the middle and late 1970s. One was the conspicuously bald Nazi war criminal in *Marathon Man*. A concentration camp dentist adept at removing gold from Jewish teeth, he attacks the nerve ends of Dustin Hoffman's molars to extract information. This study of cold, implacable evil conjured up every nightmare one has ever had about a Demon Dentist. In contrast (almost, it seems, an act of expiation), in *The Boys From Brazil* he transformed himself into the elderly Jewish avenger, a character obviously based on Simon Wiesenthal, the man who tracked down Eichman. Gaunt and obsessional in his search for Nazi persecutors, Olivier went, as always, deep under the skin of the part. His soft-spoken, self-effacing 'Wiesenthal' is another in his gallery of intensely felt impersonations.

There have been a few mistakes, of course – *The Power and The Glory*, *The Betsy*, *The Jazz Singer* – but even with years of experience it is never possible to be sure that 'the set-up' is foolproof. How can you guard against being taken for a ride (literally) when you are put on a wobbling bicycle in shirt sleeves and braces in a piffling comedy like *A Little Romance*. You just have to put up with a critic asking: 'Is this worthy of the finest Richard III and Othello of our generation?'

If you are the director, then your responsibility is

considerably greater; so, on a very different plane, I think it is fair to question a sequence which Olivier allowed in the screen version of *Three Sisters* in 1970. As well as playing the old doctor, Chebutikin, he directed it with the fine cast from the National Theatre production. In practically every way this was a lovely piece of work, but it seemed to me there was one serious flaw. To open out the stage play, he interpolated a dream sequence in which Irina imagines herself in Moscow. When the idea was conceived it probably seemed a pleasant flight of fancy. But the special poignancy of those three Chekhov sisters buried deep in the country is that they *never* reach the Moscow of which they talk endlessly. To show this hope fulfilled – even as a dream – was a disruptive mistake which destroyed the claustrophobic mood.

Films and video tapes guarantee that a considerable body of Olivier's most important stage work is now preserved. As well as five major Shakespeare roles (Henry V, Hamlet, Richard III, Shylock and Lear) we have a permanent record of his James Tyrone in Eugene O'Neill's *Long Day's Journey into Night* (stage 1971, television 1973). They also make it possible to see him in a number of exceptional parts that he never did on the stage.

These stretch back to his Orlando in the 1936 *As You Like It*, though it would be a kindness not to revive the faintly comic, and now virtually inaudible, version available today. We have his Macheath (*The Beggar's Opera*, 1952), John Gabriel Borkman in Ibsen's play (his first television part, in 1958), Big Daddy (*Cat on a Hot Tin Roof*, television 1976) the alcoholic husband (*Come Back Little Sheba*, television 1977) and his memorable blind old lawyer (*A Voyage Round My Father*, television 1982).

Long before the days of the cinema, the American actor Edwin Booth defined acting as the work of 'a sculptor who carves in snow'. This formidable array of films means that many of Olivier's performances will never melt away.

Twelve

Last Exits

In the early 1970s Olivier faced a number of harassing problems. Though cancer was cured, a series of debilitating illnesses followed. Unknown to the public he was also the victim of an actor's most dreaded fear: the inability to remember lines which lead to an almost continual state of stage fright. Another canker was the knowledge that moves were going on behind the scenes to end his directorship of the National.

Most of these crises he weathered very well. The difficulty with lines prevented him taking on any big new part for three years, but this was partially disguised by appearances in films. He was able to continue in plays already firmly in the National repertoire. He led the company to Los Angeles. Exchanging motley for ermine, he took his seat in the House of Lords and in his maiden speech referred to the theatre, in a favourite phrase of his, as 'the first glamourizer of thought'. If he cut down on his stage acting, he increased his work as a director. Literally during breaks from hospital treatment, he was directing *The Three Sisters*. The Chekhov play along with *The Crucible* and *Juno and the Paycock*, which he staged a little earlier, were three of the National's most outstanding productions.

Actors always say they enjoy working in a play under Olivier because he is what they call an actor's director. He appreciates their problems. He sees exactly what help they need. And he knows the best way to give advice. They find it particularly useful that he has the play completely 'blocked out' with all the moves decided when they arrive for the first rehearsal. This is in welcome contrast to many younger directors who work on the principle that moves should evolve by instinct.

Though he does not unduly interfere while rehearsals are in progress, he expects actors to show courage because he has never been afraid of taking chances with his interpretation of a character. If actors lacking his technique try to duck out from something he has suggested, or for some personal reason don't want to do it that way, he can be insistent, and has an awkward habit of slipping in during a run to see they haven't jettisoned it while his back was turned. Some directors verge on the sadistic, but Olivier is never unpleasant to an actor in front of the rest of the cast unless he is young, defiant and unwisely tries to argue. Then the hooded eyelids come down, the voice rasps. Normally people who aren't managing what he wants are just taken quietly to one side after rehearsal.

As an actor, he cannot resist jumping up on the stage to show exactly how he wants something done, and one danger for younger actors is that they will catch his distinctive inflections. Over the years we have seen quite a few 'little Oliviers', either admiring imitators or unable to avoid catching his vocal mannerisms.

With a feeling of absolute confidence in their director, the cast is carried firmly along in rehearsal until a most sensitive orchestration has been achieved and every member of the company feels himself integrated into an ensemble. All of which they find particularly pleasing because it is done without affectation and without elaborate theorising. Older players especially appreciate Olivier's basic attitude: get on and do it, don't talk about it.

In 1970, the same year that he took *Three Sisters* to America and received his peerage, Olivier embarked on his first important new part since *The Dance of Death*. His Shylock in Jonathan Miller's production of *The Merchant of Venice* had all the Olivier ingredients: a fresh, highly original approach to the character; a performance of great panache; and a make-up of unusual subtlety. With the play set in the 1880s he was able to break the conception of Shylock as a monster (as the part used to be played) or as a racial martyr (the sympathetic modern approach). Instead we were confronted by a rich cosmopolitan merchant in morning coat and twirling a cane. Instead of a hooked nose, he changed his appearance with a prominent row of teeth and a protruding lower lip to give a Semitic look. Hebraic intonations were concealed under an accent obviously acquired at Eton with dropped 'Gs' suggesting holidays spent with the English huntin' crowd and week-ends at Tranby Croft.

'Many a time and oft in the Rialto . . .' was spoken slyly over the top of a newspaper in which he was reading the shipping intelligence through pince-nez. He executed a little dance like a happy school boy on hearing of Antonio's losses at sea. This good humour and playing against the lines could of course only be sustained for a while. Urbanity had to turn to animal savagery when he came to the plea: 'If you prick us, do we not bleed?' Half storming, half throwing the speech away, Olivier obviously had a problem in changing the mood. Afterwards, it was difficult to return to the personality of the Victorian clubman. His final subjection was deeply felt, but even if, ultimately, this Shylock failed to move us, it was a reasonable price to pay for so entertaining a portrayal. Most remarkably this performance released him from the prison of his fears, the stage fright which for five and a half years he recalled as 'agonising dread': Dr Miller seems to have acted as not only his director but his psychiatrist.

The next year he was ready to take on yet another role – James Tyrone in Eugene O'Neill's stark autobiographical drama *Long Day's Journey into Night*. Tyrone is based on James O'Neill, the author's Irish father, and Olivier sank himself into the character of the neurotic and miserly actor. Morose, yet endearingly grandiloquent, Tyrone was to be one of his finest parts. His small self-satisfied sniff after quoting Shakespeare; his reeling drunken step back off a table; the moment of terrible weariness: all were beautifully done.

This haunting production was cheered by a first night audience unaware that the star was keeping further illness at bay and fighting a rearguard action against surrendering his job. Recurring ill-health meant that a change in the directorship of the National could not be long forestalled. At last, reluctantly and informally, Olivier himself admitted that he could not continue. But it is one thing to say it, quite another actually to go. It was difficult to make a clean break and to accept a successor even as sympathetic as Peter Hall. Everything in an actor's make-up demands bringing a part to a climax; so with life. Not to open the new theatre was very hard to accept.

He played just two more parts at the National. With a hint of his old calculated humility, Olivier brought his regime to an end not in a major classical role but in the kind of small character part in which he revels: Antonio, the eccentric grandfather in Eduardo de Filippo's Neapolitan comedy *Saturday Night, Sunday Morning*. As the old tailor who enjoys senile pranks and is for ever snatching people's hats to iron them, he gave a performance full of quirky gestures and flashes of absurdity.

There was a delicious moment when he seized the brown trilby of a visiting doctor and pretended to put it on a chair; but this was only a feint, and with a look of wicked triumph he hurried away with his trophy to the ironing board. If he felt resentment that he had – as he thought – been unceremoniously released by the board of directors, it was smothered in his relish of the part. Seven weeks later he was formally replaced, but there was one final role to be played, that of John Tagg, venerable Glasgwegian labour leader in a talkative political piece called *The Party*. A great many earnest people sat around in a Kensington flat arguing into the early hours. Olivier was called on to do very little until near the end. Then he delivered a speech of about twenty minutes in which he argued the need for proletarian action versus intellectual theory. To memorise so long a monologue was a tremendous feat at that time. He managed it over four months, getting up at seven most mornings and dividing the script into ten-line paragraphs, each of which took some four hours to learn. In a crumpled suit, Olivier gave the tangled words as much variety and fire as was consistent with a cloth-capped old party warhorse who had spent his life on the barricades.

As Tagg, he appeared at the Old Vic for the last time – took his final bow there as an actor – on 21 March, 1974. There was a speech from Peter Hall and a great ovation from an audience who rose to their feet. He has not been on the stage since, and one is reluctant to accept this as the final memory of a great actor in the theatre. After the performance I recall driving back over Waterloo Bridge in the winter gloom looking at the still dark and uncompleted shell of the National Theatre, and trying to visualise it blazing with lights, a year or so hence.

We had every reason then to expect that we should be streaming out of the new theatre after a first night on which Laurence Olivier had fulfilled his hopes and his destiny and brought his career to a triumphant climax as King Lear. That was the plan. But unfortunately life is often a pale imitation of drama. As we know, this vision was never to materialise. He had to take what comfort he could from having one of the three theatres in the South Bank complex named after him and to make the speech of welcome to the Queen at the official opening in October 1976.

As it has turned out, we have not been entirely cheated of his Lear, and for this we have to thank television. Last year Granada produced an impressive version, finely directed by Michael Elliott, which has won awards in America and was shown at the White House after a dinner given by the Reagans to Olivier and his wife. It is a brave, memorable performance, showing a mind keenly at work even if there is not the once huge reservoir of strength on which to rely.

I think we can see how the actor decided to tackle this great blasted oak of a part in which he had been so unfaltering and unflagging at the height of his powers nearly forty years before. Then he had what was described as 'the creative stamina' to rise to every phase the role demands. Now he knew that he needed to scale it down to what he could physically and vocally encompass. He would give us more the 'foolish fond old man' less the imperious tyrant. His greatest gift to the part was that he had reached an age' where he could draw on personal experiences of a long life. He had achieved greatness, but had also known pain and sorrow. He understood the anger and hurt (so acutely felt by Lear) at betrayal by those you love.

When he divides his kingdom this mild, sweet Lear could well be, like the actor, in the aftermath of illness. There is a gentle sadness in his eye and he gives vent only occasionally to subdued bursts of his once-fearful rage. We are more than usually conscious of the self-pitying reiteration that he is a poor old man. This benign reading works well until his furious attack on Regan and Goneril ('you unnatural hags') when the actor cannot summon up enough guns. Nor is his evocation of the 'all-shaking thunder' of the storm on the heath the mighty crack it should be. But though he cannot rise to his previous heights here, Olivier returns to form in the later mad scenes when, garlanded in flowers, his encounter with the blinded Gloucester has a singular sweetness. Lear has found tranquility again and touches of irony and a roguish sense of fun suggest a vein of sanity under surface madness.

When he was younger, Olivier painted heavy lines of age on his face. Now old, his complexion appears curiously pink and smooth; it is as if there is a child's face under the white beard giving him a look of extraordinary innocence. And this fusion of age and youth is particularly moving when, in the last scene, he carries in the body of the dead Cordelia. Tenderly he places her on a flat rock and gently lays his snow-white head on her breast as he dies. The camera pulls back leaving them – old man and young daughter – sweet babes peaceful and reconciled in death. It is an unforgettable ending.

I would like to leave Olivier with this poignant tableau in my mind, but must briefly fill in the years since he left the National. He had been indomitable, simply declining to accept age or illness. Unable to continue in the theatre, he concentrated on the cinema and television. *Sleuth, Marathon Man, The Boys From Brazil* and several others have already been mentioned. In one single year, 1976, he made three films for the cinema and three for television. His total between 1975 and today is twenty, of which two have yet to be shown.

In 1980 he directed Joan Plowright in her earlier London success *Filumena* on Broadway; firmly declining a 'ghost' he set about writing his autobiography *Confessions of an Actor*, a work of sometimes alarming frankness; when a kidney operation forced him to slow down and postpone a television play, he promptly announced he was starting *Olivier on Acting* which we hope will be a text book to set beside Stanislavsky's *An Actor Prepares*.

It is hardly surprising that his wife observes with admiring exasperation that he was never destined to lead an ordinary life. 'If he just existed from day to day without any purpose he would be lost', she says, and he chimes in, 'I am a workman – therefore I work. If I stopped I would cut my throat.'

Thirteen

Curtain Call

Looking back over a career which spans sixty years and which he shows very little inclination to ease into benign retirement, it is interesting to consider whether Laurence Olivier has lived up to the qualities he once defined as necessary for a successful actor.

First he named talent as something basic which must be developed into skill. Next he put luck and the ability at the right moment to seize the opportunities which luck provides. Stamina he held to be another vital ingredient of success, and this he certainly possessed in abundance until his mid-sixties after which he substituted endurance.

There are several other gifts which he does not specify: originality, showmanship and humour. But these have been part of his equipment as has the most indefinable of all: star-quality. There is one other precept absent from his list, probably because he would have to admit he had not followed it: a determination not to be diverted from the main stream of achievement by alluring irrelevancies. Because of his versatility, and his involvement in nearly every aspect of theatre and cinema, Olivier has sacrified a certain amount of precious time which might have been better devoted simply to acting.

There are a great many major parts in which we would dearly have liked to see him. His Shakespearean gallery lacks Prospero, Richard II, Angelo, Benedick, Petruchio and one or two more besides. He gave us only one stage Hamlet and his only Brutus was as a boy. Of all the towering heroes of Greek tragedy he took on only Oedipus. How did he resist Tamburlaine and Faustus and fail to bring his quizzical humour to any of Ben Jonson's rogues? Why no Tartuffe – or any Molière? In Chekhov he has never played Vershinin, Gayev or Tregorin, all of whom would have suited him perfectly. Even more strangely, Olivier passed up Wilde, most of Ibsen and nearly all Shaw.

Of course, the achievements far outweigh the losses. But it is fair to ask whether Olivier should sometimes have shown more seriousness of mind. If he had possessed less flair and virtuosity might he not have concentrated on a number of more solid parts? He has not had the dogged resolve of other – lesser – actors. No doubt some of these roles were not played simply because the opportunities to do them did not present themselves at the right moment. Also he has never much cared about playing parts in which other actors have enjoyed recent success. This was not because he feared comparison – he would have wiped the stage with most of them – but because duplication seemed dull.

Because he has so consistently wanted to do the unusual, Olivier may well have turned down parts which lacked that last degree of excitement to appeal to him. Some may have been postponed until too late. These may well be questions he will answer for us in the book he has promised us on acting. I hope so; though I recall that he has always been dismissive about theory. Will he be able to hold a mirror to himself and analyse his own faults and virtues?

He should be able to tell us how he has trained his voice to blow-torch power and more about the way he managed to increase its range. He has always believed that holding a pause was one of the most valuable weapons in an actor's armoury and it will be interesting if he can explain how he is able to pause longer and more effectively than any actor since – to judge by reports – Macready. Tyrone Guthrie once told him that an actor must learn to love a character he dislikes if he is to make him believable, and I hope we shall learn how he managed this with Sergius, Henry V and Shakespeare's arch-villain, Richard III.

Other personal qualities are sure to elude him. No one can define his own sex appeal or personal magnetism. Olivier is bound to find it difficult to discuss what has been called his 'ability to communicate a sense of danger'. He has an eye which can sweep an audience, pause and hold us mesmerised. This may be calculated but appears intuitive. But his refusal to rely on acting clichés to create ready-made effects and instead to substitute unpredictability is possibly his most fascinating quality of all. We watch him never knowing what he will do next

– whisper or explode. Sometimes the explosion may be arbitrary, like a schoolmaster keeping a class awake, but it always seems right.

So we come back to the question raised at the start about whether Olivier is the greatest actor of our time. That he has made occasional mistakes in choice of plays and given a few overwrought performances should not go against him. If you climb as high as he has, the smallest slip seems a big fall. What is indisputable is that no other actor of his generation has given audiences such a range of Shakespearean performances and endowed each so splendidly: virile Hamlet, demoniac Richard, volcanic Othello, boulevardier Shylock, sweet Lear, dynamic Hotspur, quavering Shallow, upstart Malvolio, horror-surfeited Titus, power-accumulating Macbeth, full-throttle Romeo, blisteringly contemptuous Coriolanus, and a Henry V who really made men feel that they would hold their manhood cheap to be not with him upon Saint Crispin's day.

To these add his frenzied Captain Edgar, raucous Archie Rice, wistful Astrov; recall the laughter raised by his absurdly arrogant Sergius, amorous Mr Tattle, blustering Captain Brazen. To possess the technique (to say nothing of the leg and heart) to bring all these parts to life means astonishing versatility. One is tempted to stray into even wider speculation: to ask if in any age any other actor has possessed such ability to play mighty tragedy and coax so much fun out of comedy. But that's more matter for another May morning.

Select Theatre and Film Chronology

1917   **Julius Caesar**. First public appearance aged 10 as Brutus. *All Saints Choir School, Marylebone, London.*

1925   **Henry VIII**. Walk on parts. *Empire Theatre.*

1926   **The Farmer's Wife**. *Birmingham Repertory Company tour.*

1927   **She Stoops to Conquer** (Tony Lumpkin), **Uncle Vanya** (Vanya), **The Silver Box**, **All's Well that Ends Well** (Parolles), **The Adding Machine**, **Bird in Hand**. All at *Birmingham Repertory Theatre.*

1928   **Journey's End** (Stanhope), Director: James Whale. Sunday night performance, *Apollo.*

1929   **Beau Geste**. Director: Basil Dean. *His Majesty's.* **The Circle of Chalk**. Director: Basil Dean. *New Theatre.* **Murder on the Second Floor**. Director: William Mollison. *Eltinge Theatre, New York* (Olivier's first visit to America).

1930   **Private Lives**. Director: Noel Coward. *Phoenix Theatre.* **Too Many Crooks**. (Olivier's first film) Director: George King. **The Temporary Widow** (Anglo-German film). Director: Gustav Ucicky.

1931   **Private Lives**. *Times Square Theatre, New York.* **Friends and Lovers** (RKO. Olivier's first Hollywood film). Director: Victor Schertzinger. **The Yellow Passport** (20th Century-Fox film). Director: Raoul Walsh.

1932   **Westward Passage** (RKO film). Director: Robert Milton with Ann Harding. **Perfect Understanding** (United Artists film). Director: Cyril Gardner, with Gloria Swanson.

1933   **Rats of Norway**, *Playhouse Theatre*. Director: Raymond Massey. **The Green Bay Tree**. Director: Jed Harris, *Court Theatre, New York.*

1934	**Biography**. Director Noel Coward, *Globe Theatre*. **Queen of Scots**. Director John Gielgud, *New Theatre*. **Theatre Royal**. Director: Noel Coward, *Lyric Theatre*.
1935	**Golden Arrow**, Director: Laurence Olivier, with Greer Garson, *Whitehall Theatre*. **Romeo and Juliet**, Director: John Gielgud, *New Theatre*. **Moscow Nights**, (film) Director: Anthony Asquith.
1936	**Bees on the Boatdeck**. *Lyric Theatre*. **As You Like It**, (film) Director: Paul Czinner, with Elisabeth Bergner. **Fire Over England** (film), Director: William K. Howard, with Vivien Leigh.
1937	*Old Vic Season:* **Hamlet**. Director: Tyrone Guthrie. **Twelfth Night**. Director Tyrone Guthrie. **Henry V**. Director: Tyrone Guthrie. **Twenty-One Days** (London Films). Director: Basil Dean, with Vivien Leigh. **The Divorce of Lady X** (London Films). Director: Tim Whelan, with Merle Oberon.
1937-38	*Old Vic Season* **Macbeth**. Director: Michel Saint-Denis. **Othello**. Director: Tyrone Guthrie. **Coriolanus**. Director: Lewis Casson.
1938	**Q Planes** (London Films). Director: Tim Whelan.
1939	**No Time for Comedy**. Director: Guthrie McClintic, *Ethel Barrymore Theatre, New York*. **Wuthering Heights** (United Artists film). Director: William Wyler. **Rebecca** (United Artists film), Director: Alfred Hitchcock.
1940	**Romeo and Juliet**. Director: Laurence Olivier, with Vivien Leigh, *51st Street Theatre, New York*. **Pride and Prejudice**. (MGM film) Director: Robert Z. Leonard. **Lady Hamilton** (London Films). Director: Alexander Korda, with Vivien Leigh.
1941	**49th Parallel** (Film), Director: Michael Powell.
1943	**The Demi-Paradise** (Two Cities film), Director: Anthony Asquith.

1943-44	Henry V (Two Cities film), Producer and Director: Laurence Olivier.
1944	*Old Vic Season at the New Theatre:* **Peer Gynt.** Director: Tyrone Guthrie.**Arms and the Man,** Director: John Burrell. **Richard III.** Director: John Burrell
1945	**Uncle Vanya.** Director: John Burrell. Directed **The Skin of our Teeth,** with Vivien Leigh.
1945-46	*Second Old Vic Season at the New Theatre:* **Henry IV, Part I.** Director: John Burrell. **Henry IV, Part II.** Director: John Burrell. **Oedipus Rex.** Director: Michel Saint-Denis. **The Critic.** Director: Miles Malleson.
1946	Hotspur, Shallow, Oedipus, Mr. Puff and Astrov in Old Vic Company season at the *Century Theatre, New York.* **King Lear.** Director: Laurence Olivier, Old Vic production at the *New Theatre.*
1947	Directed **Born Yesterday,** *Garrick Theatre.* **Hamlet** (Two Cities film). Producer and Director: Laurence Olivier.
1948	*Tour of Australia and New Zealand with Old Vic Company.* **The School for Scandal.** Director: Laurence Olivier. **The Skin of Our Teeth.** Director: Laurence Olivier.**Richard III.** Director: John Burrell.
1949	*Old Vic Season at the New Theatre.* **The School for Scandal.** Director: Laurence Olivier. **Richard III.** Director: John Burrell. **Antigone.** Director: Laurence Olivier. Directed **A Streetcar Named Desire,** *Aldwych Theatre.*
1950	**Venus Observed.** Director: Laurence Olivier. *St James's Theatre.* Directed: **Captain Carvallo,** *St. James's Theatre.* **Carrie** (Paramount film). Director: William Wyler.
1951	**Ceasar and Cleopatra** and **Antony and Cleopatra** Director: Michael Benthall. *St. James's Theatre.* Both productions at *Ziegfeld Theatre, New York.*

The Magic Box (British Lion Film) Director: John Boulting.

1952 Directed **Venus Observed,** *New Century Theatre New York.* **The Beggar's Opera** (British Lion film). Director: Peter Brook.

1953 **The Sleeping Prince.** Director: Laurence Olivier, *Phoenix Theatre.*

1954 **Richard III** (London Films) Director: Laurence Olivier.

1955 *Season at the Shakespeare Memorial Theatre, Stratford-on-Avon.*
Twelfth Night. Director: John Gielgud. **Macbeth.** Director: Glen Byam Shaw. **Titus Andronicus.** Director: Peter Brook.

1956 **The Prince and the Showgirl.** (Warner Brothers film). Director and producer: Laurence Olivier, with Marilyn Monroe.

1957 **The Entertainer.** Director: Tony Richardson, *Royal Court Theatre.* **Titus Andronicus.** Revival. Tour of Europe, and *Stoll Theatre.* **The Entertainer.** *Palace Theatre.*

1958 **The Entertainer,** *Royale Theatre, New York.* **The Devil's Disciple** (United Artists film). Director: Guy Hamilton. **John Gabriel Borkman.** (British television debut,) Director: Casper Wrede. **The Moon and Sixpence** (American television). Director: David Susskind.

1959 **Coriolanus.** Director: Peter Hall, *Stratford - on - Avon.* **Spartacus** (Universal film) Director: Stanley Kubrick. **The Entertainer** (Woodfall film). Director: Tony Richardson.

1960 Directed **The Tumbler,** *Helen Hayes Theatre, New York.* with Charlton Heston. **Rhinoceros.** Director: Orson Welles, *Royal Court Theatre.*

1961 **Beckett,** *Hudson Theatre, New York.* **The Power and the Glory** (American television). Director: Marc Daniels.

1962	*Chichester Festival Theatre:* Directed **The Chances.** **The Broken Heart.** Director: Laurence Olivier. **Uncle Vanya.** Director: Laurence Olivier. **Semi-Detached.** Director: Tony Richardson, *Saville Theatre.* **Term of Trial** (Warner Bros. film). Director: Peter Glenville.
1963	*National Theatre opened at the Old Vic:* Directed **Hamlet.** with Peter O'Toole. **Uncle Vanya.** Director: Laurence Olivier. **The Recruiting Officer.** Director: William Gaskill. **Uncle Vanya** (film). Director: Stuart Burge.
1964	**Othello.** Director: John Dexter, *Old Vic.* **The Master Builder.** Director: Peter Wood, *Old Vic.*
1965	Directed **The Crucible,** *Old Vic.* **Othello.** Director: Peter Wood, *Old Vic.* **Love for Love.** Director: Peter Wood, *Old Vic.* **Bunny Lake is Missing** (Columbia film). Director: Otto Preminger. **Othello** (film). Director: Stuart Burge. **Khartoum** (United Artists film). Director: Basil Dearden.
1966	Directed **Juno and the Paycock,** *Old Vic.*
1967	**The Dance of Death.** Director: Glen Byam Shaw, *Old Vic.* Directed: **Three Sisters,** *Old Vic.* **Love for Love, The Dance of Death** and **A Flea in her Ear** in the National Theatre Company tour of Canada.
1968	Directed **Love's Labour Lost,** *Old Vic.* **The Shoes of the Fisherman** (MGM film). Director: Michael Anderson. **Oh! What a Lovely War** (film) Director: Richard Attenborough. **The Dance of Death** (film) Director: David Giles.
1969	**Home and Beauty.** Director: Frank Dunlop, *Old Vic.* **The Dance of Death** revival, *Old Vic.* **The Battle of Britain** (United Artists film). Director: Guy Hamilton. **David Copperfield** (film) Director: Delbert Mann.. **Three Sisters** (British Lion film) Director: Laurence Olivier.
1970	**Three Sisters** and **The Beaux' Stratagem** in Los Angeles. **The Merchant of Venice.** Director: Jonathan Miller, *Old Vic.*

1971	Directed **Amphitryon 38**, *New Theatre*. **Long Day's Journey into Night.** Director: Michael Blakemore, *New Theatre*. **Nicholas and Alexandra** (Columbia film). Director: Franklin J. Schaffner. **Lady Caroline Lamb** (EMI film). Director: Robert Bolt.
1972	**Sleuth** (Fox-Rank film). Director: Joesph L Mankiewicz. **Long Day's Journey into Night** (television film).
1973	**Saturday, Sunday, Monday.** Director: Franco Zeffirelli, *Old Vic*. **The Party.** Director: John Dexter, *Old Vic*. **The Merchant of Venice** (telelvision film). Director: Jonathan Miller.
1974	Directed **Eden End**, *Old Vic*.
1975	**Love Among the Ruins** (telvision film). Director: George Cukor, with Katharine Hepburn. **The Seven Per Cent Solution** (Universal film). Director: Hebert Ross.
1976	**Marathon Man** (Paramount film). Director: John Schlesinger. **The Life of Jesus Christ** (television film). Director: Franco Zeffirelli. **A Bridge Too Far** (Joseph E. Levine film). Director: Richard Attenborough. **The Collection** (British television). Director: Michael Apted. **Cat on a Hot Tin Roof** (British television). Director: Robert Moore. Olivier's first television direction **Hindle Wakes** (British television).
1977	**The Betsy** (United Artists film). Director: Daniel Petrie. **Come Back Little Sheba** (British television) Director: Silvio Narizzano.
1978	**The Boys from Brazil** (film) Director: F.J. Schaffner.
1979	**A Little Romance** (film). Director: George Roy Hill. **Dracula** (film). Director: John Badham.
1980	Directed **Filumena**, *St James Theatre New York*. **The Jazz Singer** (film) Director: Richard Fleischer.
1981	**Brideshead Revisited** (British television) Director: Charles Sturridge.

94

himself in the position of a grey-headed Scottish statesman forced to recognize what he cannot approve of:

> O would, or I had seen the day
>   That treason thus could sell us,
> My auld grey head had lien in clay,   old lain
>   Wi' BRUCE and loyal WALLACE!
> But pith and power, till my last hour,   but with all my strength
>   I'll mak this declaration;
> We're bought and sold for English gold,
>   Such a parcel of rogues in a nation!

Once again, the movement of the tune dictates his arrangement of words and clauses. In the final four lines, for instance, emphasis is placed on 'this declaration' and on 'Such a parcel of rogues in a nation'. The song has been written with performance and the listener in mind throughout. A large part of its art consists in the accuracy with which it satisfies the demanding technical requirements of the chosen melody while helping to give it a new dimension of meaning.

In contrast to songs expressing serious sentiment, a number of the lyrics Burns supplied for volume four of the *Museum* are devoted to the creation of laughter. Given Burns's ready wit and ability to invent comedy of character and of situation in his poems, as well as in songs printed in earlier volumes of the collection, this is no surprise.

Drawing on a tradition of derisive vernacular personal name-calling and description, he is at his most mischievous in two songs about married couples who are at odds. In each case, it seems certain that the chosen melody helps to account for Burns's use of a particularly fast and nimble Lowland Scots. In 'Willie Wastle', he heaps one abusive item on top of another in his portrait of the unfortunate wife, daughter of 'tinkler Madgie', so that she is made to seem truly grotesque. There is a close match between the jaunty pace of the tune and the use of

an unusually large number of homely Scots words: the
song is an in-joke for those who understand its
vocabulary. This is very much in keeping with one kind of
country tradition. 'The bairns gat out wi' an unco shout'
differs in that the initial point of view this time is that of a
frustrated wife, commenting on her impotent elderly
husband:

paddles	He paidles out, and he paidles in
	And he paidles late and early, O!
lain	This seven lang years I hae lien by his
	side,
pithless old man	An' he is but a fusionless carlie, O.

Once again, Burns makes use of the vernacular to bring
out the comedy of marital discord ('paidles . . . fusion-
less carlie . . . feirrie auld wife'). Here, incidentally, he
touches on the theme of feeble sexual performance,
subject — like its opposite — of a number of songs in
'The Merry Muses of Caledonia', a lively collection of his
own bawdy songs and those of others which Burns was
proud of but which, given the censorship of the age, he
did not seek to print.[14]

The best known of all the humorous songs in volume 4
offers proof that Burns the exciseman kept his sense of
humour to the end, despite work pressures and the pull of
officialdom. He has matched his verbal skills to a tune —
marked 'With spirit' in the *Museum* — which sets the heels
tapping. The words of 'The deil cam fiddlin thro' the
town' seem to skip along merrily, for:

	There's threesome reels, there's foursome
	reels,
	There's hornpipes and strathspeys, man,
one ever came	But the ae best dance e'er cam to the
	Land
devil's away with	Was, the deil's awa wi' th' Exciseman.

'The deil cam fiddlin thro' the town' communicates two

of Burns's finest and most characteristic qualities, from which much else flowed, a love of pure melody, and the ability to laugh at life.

NOTES

 1. Note on 'To the weaver's gin ye go', *Notes on Scottish Song by Robert Burns*, ed. James C. Dick (1908), p. 24.
 2. *Letters of Robert Burns*, II, 306.
 3. Hugh MacDiarmid, *Burns Today And Tomorrow* (Edinburgh, 1959), p. 33.
 4. *Poems And Songs of Robert Burns*, ed. James Kinsley (Oxford, 1968), vol. 3, p. 1022.
 5. *Letters*, II, 336.
 6. *Letters*, II, 328.
 7. *Notes On Scottish Song by Robert Burns*, p. 52.
 8. *Letters*, I, *passim:* (August 1787-February 1788).
 9. *Letters*, I, 101.
10. David Herd, *Scottish Songs*, 1776, vol. 2, p. 221.
11. *Letters*, II, 242, September 1793 to George Thomson.
12. Text from *Poems And Songs of Robert Burns* ed. James Kinsley, vol. II, pp. 700-701.
13. *Scots Musical Museum*, IV (1792), nos. 351, 347, 360, 386, 378, 376, 399.
14. See *The Merry Muses of Caledonia*, ed. James Barke and S. G. Smith (Edinburgh, 1959, rpt. 1982.).

REPUTATION

Burns has never lacked admirers. Any summary account of his reputation must begin by acknowledging that he was recognized on the first appearance of the Kilmarnock edition in 1786 as a poet of quite exceptional ability. His inventiveness, mastery of sentiment, and bent for satire were all welcomed and praised. A number of leading Scottish men of letters did their best to assist him, partly by subscribing to an enlarged edition of *Poems, Chiefly In the Scottish Dialect*. A complicating factor, however, was that Burns's emergence from rural obscurity seemed to satisfy eighteenth-century primitivist theory — the preconception that poetic genius and lack of formal education went together. This led to false expectations, as well as to some plain misreading of what he had written. Then there was the tendency of some Scots to believe that Burns should write more poems of a genteel kind in English, turning his back on the vernacular which was his main strength. Dr John Moore, for instance, who undoubtedly meant well but did not really understand the nature of Burns's originality, seems to have wanted the poet to produce a latter-day equivalent to Vergil's *Georgics*, in English verse.

Inevitably, the contemporary reception of Burns's work coloured subsequent accounts. By a curious set of ironies connected with inherited prejudices about a 'hierarchy' of literary kinds — and also with the early publishing history of Burns's poetry — his songs did not figure largely in written comment, even although they were extremely popular when sung. A misleading assumption tended to be made that song was somehow trivial or insignificant in comparison with odes and other classically recognised types of poem.

Two hundred years after the original appearance of the Kilmarnock edition, the consequences of this particular bias in criticism remain with us. Thanks largely to the pioneering efforts of James Dick, editor of *The Songs of Robert Burns* (1903), a comprehensive three volume edition by James Kinsley of the *Poems and Songs* (Oxford, 1968), and individual contributions by such critics as David Daiches and Thomas Crawford, Burns's achievement in song now belatedly receives as much attention as the poetry, but there is still a good deal of leeway to make up. It is only within recent years that recorded song performance has begun to make possible fresh critical work on the songs, linking words and melody in a single unity.

With regard to the poems, an obvious challenge is to consider Burns's work in a continuum which includes Hugh MacDiarmid in the twentieth century. Too often, assessment of Burns has been made exclusively in terms of what he owed to earlier Scottish poetry; links forward to his ablest successor in Scottish poetry also deserve to be considered. Mary Ellen Brown's *Burns And Tradition* (1984) is a valuable recent study of different types of connection between the poet and oral tradition. Beyond Scotland, it is time for fuller recognition in mainstream Anglo-American criticism and education of the significance of Burns's work. *Poems, Chiefly In The Scottish Dialect* ranks in quality and importance with Blake's *Songs of Innocence and Experience* (1794) and with *Lyrical Ballads* (1798); but a survey of college and university syllabuses, or of published criticism, would reveal a gross imbalance in favour of the English poets in this group.

SELECT BIBLIOGRAPHY

The Poems And Songs of Robert Burns, ed. James Kinsley, 3 vols. (Oxford, 1968).

The Kilmarnock Poems (Poems, Chiefly In The Scottish Dialect, 1786), ed. Donald A. Low (London, 1985).

The Songs of Robert Burns, Now First Printed With The Melodies For Which They Were Written, ed. James C. Dick (London, 1903).

The Merry Muses of Caledonia, ed. James Barke and S. G. Smith (Edinburgh, 1959; rpt. 1982).

The Letters of Robert Burns, ed. J. De Lancey Ferguson and G. Ross Roy, 2 vols. (Oxford, 1985).

Robert Burns's Commonplace Book, 1783-85, ed. J. C. Ewing and D. Cook [Glasgow, 1938]; rpt., with introduction by D. Daiches (London, 1965).

Robert Burns's Tour of the Borders 5 May-1 June 1787, ed. Raymond Lamont Brown (Totowa, New Jersey, 1972).

Robert Burns's Tours of the Highlands and Stirlingshire 1787, ed. Raymond Lamont Brown (Ipswich), 1973.

Bibliography and Concordance

J. W. Egerer, *A Bibliography of Robert Burns* (Edinburgh, 1964). Aims to list every significant original appearance of poetry or prose to 1802; most 'complete' editions to 1953.

J. B. Reid, *A Complete Word and Phrase Concordance To The Poems and Songs of Robert Burns* (Glasgow, 1889; rpt. New York, 1968).

Biography and Criticism

Mary Ellen Brown, *Burns And Tradition* (London, 1984).

Thomas Crawford, *Burns: A Study of The Poems and Songs* (Edinburgh, 1960, rpt. 1978).

Thomas Crawford, *Society and The Lyric. A Study of the Song Culture of Eighteenth-century Scotland* (Edinburgh, 1979).

David Daiches, *Robert Burns* (1950, rev. 1966, rpt. 1981).

David Daiches, *Robert Burns and His World* (London, 1971).

Catarina Ericson-Roos, *The Songs of Robert Burns: A Study of the Unity of Poetry and Music* (Uppsala, 1977).

R. D. S. Jack and Andrew Noble, eds. *The Art of Robert Burns* (London and Totowa, New Jersey, 1982).

Maurice Lindsay, *The Burns Encyclopaedia*, 3rd edition (London, 1980).

Donald A. Low, ed. *Robert Burns: The Critical Heritage* (London and Boston, 1974).

Donald A. Low, ed. *Critical Essays on Robert Burns* (London and Boston, 1974).

Carol McGuirk, *Robert Burns and the Sentimental Era* (Athens, Georgia, 1985).

David Murison, *The Guid Scots Tongue* (Edinburgh, 1977).

Franklyn B. Snyder, *The Life of Robert Burns* (New York, 1932; reprinted Hamden, Conn., 1968).

John Strawhorn, ed. *Ayrshire In The Time of Robert Burns* (Ayr, 1959).

Map

Armstrongs' Map of Ayrshire (1775), in six sheets. Facsimile published by Ayrshire Archaeological and Natural History Society.

Cassettes

Burns Songs from 'The Scots Musical Museum' Sung by Jean Redpath, I SRCM 157, II SCRM 162, III SCRM 163. Scottish Records, Brig o' Turk, Perthshire.